The Joy of Faithful
and
Cheerful Giving

THE JOY OF FAITHFUL AND CHEERFUL GIVING

Vincent Onyebuchi Nwankpa, Ph.D

Copyright © 2024 By Vincent Onyebuchi Nwankpa Ph.D

All rights reserved. No part of this publication may be reproduced, distributed, or transmitted in any form or by any means, including photocopying, recording, or other electronic or mechanical methods, without the prior written permission of the copyright owner and the publisher, except in the case of brief quotations embodied in critical reviews and certain other noncommercial uses permitted by copyright law. For permission requests, write to the publisher, addressed "Attention: Permissions Coordinator," at the address below.

ARPress
45 Dan Road Suite 5
Canton, MA 02021

Hotline: 1(888) 821-0229
Fax: 1(508) 545-7580

Ordering Information:

Quantity sales. Special discounts are available on quantity purchases by corporations, associations, and others. For details, contact the publisher at the address above.

Printed in the United States of America.

ISBN-13:   Softcover   979-8-89356-965-0
           eBook   979-8-89356-966-7

Library of Congress Control Number: 2024910079

Table Of Contents

Foreword iii
Blog entry v
Preface ix
Acknowledgments xi
Introduction xiii

Chapter 1 Old Testament Giving Principles 1
Chapter 2 The Motives and Purposes of Christian Giving 13
Chapter 3 The Principles and Methods of Christian Giving 31
Chapter 4 The Handicaps of Christian Giving in Many Societies 61
Chapter 5 Solutions to the Lack of Christian Giving 71

Appendix 79
Ways to Give 87
Bibliography 89
About the Author 95

Foreword

Forward for The Principles of Christian Giving, by Vincent Nwankpa, Ph.D.
January 17, 2021

Few subjects generate more controversy and are addressed less frequently than that of Christian giving. Seldom does the church deal honestly, or at all, with this most important aspect of a believer's discipleship in Christ. Dr. Nwankpa has sounded a clear and gracious voice in bringing this discussion to the table.

Clearly written and down-to-earth, this book deals with how things really are in the church regarding money, giving, and living a life that honors the Lord and participates in his kingdom work. Vincent has done us a great favor by providing a sound biblical perspective on giving. His research, practical wisdom, and long experience as a seasoned follower of Jesus and minister of the gospel provide solid help for local and para church leaders.

But be warned. Absorbing this book will challenge the reader's own values. Do we possess our riches, or do they possess us? One should be prepared to engage personally in order to gain the most benefit from this wonderful resource of information, perspective, and biblical insight.

As an added bonus, Dr. Nwankpa deals with how cultural contexts affect one's views and practices on giving. Focusing on his native Nigeria, readers will find his observations both interesting and motivational, regardless of where they call home.

This book provides a consistent and appropriate use of Scripture that instructs and exhorts the reader towards a life of joyful and generous giving. Along with numerous additional links to further study, the reader will be drawn into this most timely subject. I have enjoyed a deep friendship with Vincent and his family for over 30 years, and commend him for this outstanding contribution to the family of Christ.

Mick Boersma, Ph.D.
Professor Emeritus of Christian Ministry & Leadership
Talbot School of Theology
Biola University

Blog entry

For 'The Principles of Christian Giving' by Dr. Vincent Nwankpa
January 17, 2021

"That money talks, I'll not deny. I heard it once, it said 'goodbye'!" I grew up hearing this saying, and it often made me chuckle. Maybe that's because on our farm we had plenty of land and livestock, but little cash. Once I began pastoring a church, however, the humor in that little jingle began to fade.

There is little doubt that one of the great challenges for Christian leaders today is the task of securing adequate funding and other resources for ministry. There are numerous reasons for this, and brother Vincent Nwankpa does a tremendous job uncovering these and other issues in his new book, The Principles of Christian Giving. Enjoying the read, I found his research to be biblically solid, up-to-date, and relevant to today's realities.

The people in our first pastorate were generous. Even though our salary was low, they gave affection, time, energy, food, and faithful support to my wife and me as we began our ministry life together. But along the road our years in ministry have often been a financial struggle, and for most pastors and missionaries today the difficulties are a real and present danger to their health, welfare, and mission.

Kudos to Dr. Nwankpa for taking the time and energy to share biblical wisdom and a lifetime of experience to encourage and teach all of us in Christian service. You are correct, brother Vincent, when you assert that too little instruction about giving is being given in churches today. It is time for a renewed focus on the basic principles of giving and the joy that comes from living generously in the body of Christ!

Mick Boersma, Ph.D.
Professor Emeritus of Christian Ministry & Leadership
Talbot School of Theology
Biola University

In the summer of 1999, Vincent Nwankpa and his wife, Chinyere, started a school in Nigeria. There was nothing unusual about that; many people did it, every year.

But what *was* remarkable was that the Nwankpas started the school *from their home in Norwalk, California.*

And they had continued to run the school from Norwalk, with only occasional visits to Nigeria, for over twenty years now—Vincent as president and chief executive officer and Chinyere as a member of the board of directors. Under their direction, the Eternal Word Christian School in Nekede, Imo State, Nigeria, had grown from a meager beginning with 6 students to a thriving enrollment of 870, adding a secondary school, a library, a cafeteria, a science lab building, a dorm building, and I don't know what else, graduating students with high academic reputations, and, what is more important, with a great love for Jesus.

In achieving all of this, the Nwankpas had been ably assisted by Eternal Word Christian School's devoted faculty, their distinguished administration, and their sterling student body. But still, Vincent and Chinyere started the school *from their living room in Norwalk*. Does that sound easy to you? And they *run* it from there. It's the most amazing thing that anyone I knew personally had ever done.

It's so amazing that it was obviously a *God thing*; people cannot do that, only God can. Vincent and Chinyere are a testimony of what God can do when two people who are submitted to Him step out in faith.

I have been friends with the Nwankpas ever since I met Vincent at a missions' prayer meeting in La Mirada, California, in 1986. I was fortunate enough to be around when the school got started twenty- two years ago. For a few years there, I was even their pastor. I know these people, and please believe me when I tell you that they are the real thing. When it comes to giving, faith, love, and the joy that came from submitting to God's will and doing great things for His kingdom, these are two people who know what they are talking about.

I have read this book very carefully, and it has been a tremendous blessing to me. It is loaded with rich Bible passages and encouraging explanations, and with very practical suggestions about how to apply scriptural principles of giving in your own life. But what I like the most about this potent little volume is that what it teaches about giving is being lived out by Vincent and Chinyere in their own lives. The book presents what the Bible teaches, but it also was forged out of the Nwankpas' own personal experiences, and all of us can learn something from what they have to share.

It is my pleasure to introduce this wonderful couple to you in the hopes that through the important lessons of this book, their insights and experience will greatly enrich your walk with God. They certainly have enriched mine.

Jack Littlefield February 2, 2021

PREFACE

The idea of writing this book stemmed from the thesis I wrote in 1983 during my seminary years at ECWA Theological Seminary in Igbaja, Kwara State, Nigeria, entitled *The Principles of Christian Giving*. My motivation for choosing that topic came as a result of my own conviction about giving to God's work and giving to people, no matter how large or small the amount might be. I can't stomach seeing people in need without helping them out. I love giving! And I hate saying no to people, no matter what the circumstances might be. I had to be careful though because not saying no to people could be a weakness.

Two scriptural passages in particular were my bases for giving. The first was where Jesus said, "Give, and it will be given to you. They will pour into your lap a good measure—pressed down, shaken together, *and* running over. For by your standard of measure it will be measured to you in return" (Luke 6:38). When I remembered that I was only a steward of what the Lord had blessed me with, I was encouraged to give. When I gave to others, God was the one who would give back to me. I don't expect to receive back from the person I was giving to because that person might not have anything to give back to me, so I just give. In the second passage, Paul quoted the words of Jesus in connection with giving: "In everything I showed you that by working hard in this way you must help the weak and remember the words of the Lord Jesus, that He Himself said, 'It is more blessed to give than to receive.'" (Acts

20:35). The idea that it was more blessed to give than to receive had been a major guiding principle throughout my life.

A study of giving led us directly into the discovery of how God's Word applied to our lives. He challenged our commitment to give as we were commanded in the Scriptures. Let us learn to give cheerfully, "for God loves a cheerful giver" (2 Corinthians 9:7). Giving made an eternal difference. And because Jesus came to give instead of to receive, you were like Jesus when you give.

I pray that this book would lead you to consider what God said in His Word about giving and would stir your heart to give cheerfully so that what you gave, to God's work and to people in need, would have an impact for eternity.

ACKNOWLEDGMENTS

The writer seizes this opportunity to express his gratitude to all those who gave him moral and prayer support throughout his writing of this book. He is grateful to his wife, Chinyere Nwankpa, for coediting of this book. Many thanks to Chinyere for her patience and honest criticism.

He is also grateful to his son, Chidinma Paul Nwankpa, and his daughter, Chioma Favour Vin-Nwankpa, for their patience with him during the time of writing of this book. The author is especially grateful to his longtime friend for thirty-four years, his former pastor, and a current board member of Eternal Word Communication Ministries, Jack Littlefield, for the part he played in editing of this book.

I am honored to acknowledge the part that Dr. Mick Boersma played in writing one of the blogs of this book, "The Joy of Faithful and Cheerful Giving: Wonderful Principles to Embrace." May God bless you really good.

He is very grateful to the Almighty God for giving him the opportunity to write this book during this pandemic period. This challenging time has been in at least one way a blessing in disguise because it had afforded him the time to write this book on giving and to write another one on marriage and polygamy. The Lord is his strength and helper.

INTRODUCTION

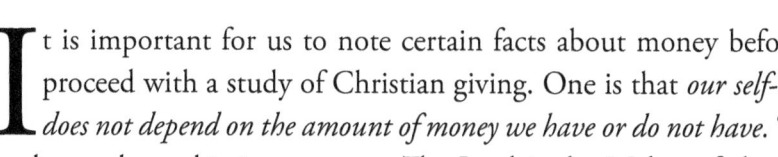

It is important for us to note certain facts about money before we proceed with a study of Christian giving. One is that *our self-worth does not depend on the amount of money we have or do not have.* "Rich and poor have this in common: The Lord is the Maker of them all" (Proverbs 22:2 NIV. See also Deuteronomy 8:16–18). The Bible teaches us that "we are God's workmanship, created in Christ Jesus to do good works, which God prepared in advance for us to do" (Ephesians 2:10 NIV). Money is not a reward for godly living. We will be rewarded when Jesus returns, and our work "will be shown for what it is because the Day will bring it to light. It will be revealed with fire, and the fire will test the quality of each man's work. If what he has built survives, he will receive his reward. If it is burned up, he will suffer loss; he himself will be saved, but only as one escaping through the flames" (1 Corinthians 3:13–15 NIV).

Another principle to keep in mind is that *money is not a guarantee of contentment.* Paul explains to us that satisfaction has nothing to do with our circumstances or material wealth: "I am not saying this because I am in need, for I have learned to be content whatever the circumstances, I know what it is to be in need, and I know what it is to have plenty. I have learned the secret of being content in any and every situation, whether well fed or hungry, whether living in plenty or want. I can do everything through Him who gives me strength" (Philippians 4:11–13 NIV). God's guidelines for success in life and true *prosperity* had nothing to do with how much money you made. Aside He instructed Joshua more than three thousand years ago, "Do not let this Book of the Law depart from your mouth; meditate on it day and night, so that you may be careful to do everything written in it. Then you will be prosperous and successful" (Joshua 1:8 NIV).

Most Christians today have learned a great deal about Christian commitment. They have learned how to surrender their lives to God or Jesus Christ. They have learned how to overcome personal weaknesses, practices, and habits which are unchristian. They uphold their commitment to attend church regularly. They have learned how to be responsible in serving in their churches. They have not overlooked their diet of devotion, private prayer, and family prayer.

But most Christians have not learned how to give, whether it is giving their money or time or talents to the Lord's work. Yet biblical giving is crucial for any Christian project, organization, business, society, or church to stand. One of the biggest problems our churches and Christian organizations face today is finances. Some of the Christians who give money for the Lord's work do it only out of compulsion: because they feel they have to. Others who give willingly do not do it cheerfully. The biblical practices of giving proportionately and giving sacrificially are rare. One reason for this is the lack of good scriptural teaching on why and how Christians should give. Although some Christians suffer from poverty, others have plenty, yet they lavish their wealth on themselves alone with no concern for the suffering masses.

I am very passionate about this topic of Christian giving, because I love to give generously, sacrificially, cheerfully, and passionately, whenever I am able. I want more people to learn to give as well. There are blessings in giving, especially when you give to those who cannot give back to you. God Almighty will be the one to reward you for having blessed others with your resources. One of the most incredible blessings of my life has been the Eternal Word Communication Ministries, which my wife and I started twenty-six years ago. Yet that ministry could never have come into being without faithful Christian people who have put into action what the Bible teaches about giving, both financially and in other ways. *When God's people practice biblical giving, great things can happen!*

Yet another important principle to remember is that *giving is the proof of love.* "If anyone has material possessions and sees his brother in need but has no pity on him, how can the love of God be in him?" (1 John 3:17). Giving to others flows from a heart of love, and the Bible, building on this truth, give clear guidelines for Spirit- led giving. One pastor from long ago said it this way:
Giving in the church can be an irritation or an inspiration. If it is done because of outward compulsion it is usually an irritation. If it comes from within and is the expression of the Christian motive it is usually an inspiration and joy.[1]

The purpose of this book is to remind God's people that they have been *bought with a price*—the blood of Jesus Christ—and that it is their responsibility to respond to God's gift by giving, according to God's principles as laid down in Scripture. "You were bought with a price; do not become slaves of men" (1 Corinthians 7:23, see also 6:19–20). Christ gave His life for you; you can in the same way give to help others.

This book will be based on both the Old and New Testaments concepts of Christian giving. Owing to the fact that the correct idea of giving is lacking in most Christians today, it is my intention to approach this work through five main divisions: Old Testament teachings on giving (tithing); the motives and purposes of Christian giving; the principles and methods of Christian giving; the handicaps of Christian giving; and finally, the solutions to the lack of Christian giving.

---

1 Albert. W. Beaven, *Putting the Church on a Full Time Basis* (New York: Doubleday, Doran and Company, Inc. 1928), p. 143.

Chapter 1

Old Testament Giving Principles

There are two kinds of giving that are consistently taught in the Scriptures: giving to the government, which is always compulsory, and giving to God which is always voluntary. Tithes were used for taxes, to funding the national budget in Israel, and not primarily for gifts to God. The Hebrew word for tithe literally means *one tenth part* or 10 percent: "Be sure to set aside a tenth of all that your fields produce each year" (Deuteronomy 14:22). The Levitical priests were responsible for collecting the tithes because Israel was a theocratic society: "When you have finished setting aside a tenth of all your produce in the third year, the year of the tithe, you shall give it to the Levite, the alien, the fatherless and the widow, so that they may eat in your towns and be satisfied" (Deuteronomy 26:12, see also 10:37–38).

The people of Israel did not pay only 10 percent. They paid other smaller taxes that were imposed on them by law, totaling an average of about 23 percent a year. All the money they paid was used to run the nation, but any giving apart from that required to run the government was purely voluntary (Exodus 25:2, 1 Chronicles 29:6–9).

Tithing Before the Law

Then Melchizedek, king of Salem, brought out bread and wine. He was priest of God Most High, and he blessed Abram, saying, "Blessed be Abram by God Most High, Creator of heaven and earth. And blessed be God Most High, who delivered your enemies into your hand." Then Abram gave him a tenth of everything (Genesis 14:18–20).

Abram gave Melchizedek, the priest of God, a tithe of what he had gained from the battle in which he defeated Kedorlaomer and brought back his nephew, Lot. This tithe included not only money and other possessions but also servants as well (Genesis 14:14–16). This tithe to Melchizedek was offered by Abram before God commanded tithing in the Old Testament Law of Moses. Abram, later known as Abraham, gave this tithe voluntarily as an appreciation for what God had done for him.

Abraham was not the only person before the Law of Moses whom the Bible connected with tithing:

> Then Jacob made a vow, saying, "If God will be with me and will watch over me on the journey I am taking and will give me food to eat and clothes to wear so that I return safely to my father's house, then the Lord will be my God and this stone that I have set up as a pillar will be God's house, and of all that you give me I will give you a tenth." (Genesis 28:20– 22)

Jacob vowed to give God 10 percent of his proceeds if God would bless him on his journey. There was nowhere in the text that God commanded Jacob to give Him a tithe. Jacob gave God his tithe voluntarily. The cases of Abraham and Jacob were the only two examples of tithing found in the Old Testament before the law was given. Brian Anderson observed the following:

> Both were examples of voluntary giving, and neither was required by God. In neither patriarch did we see an example

of tithing as a general practice of life. In fact, in Abraham's life, it appeared that we had a tithe of the spoils of military victory given to God's priest on a onetime only basis.[2]

Tithing in the Mosaic Law
There are many Old Testament passages that deal with tithing in the Mosaic law. There are verses on the herd, the flock, the produce of the land, the seed of the land, and the fruit of the tree. The Jewish people were expected to dedicate a portion of all of these products to the Lord.

A tithe of everything from the land, whether grain from the soil or fruit from the trees, belongs to the Lord; it is holy to the Lord. If a man redeems any of his tithe, he must add one fifth of the value to it. The entire tithe of the herd and flock—every tenth animal that passes under the shepherd's rod—will be holy to the Lord. He must not pick out the good from the bad or make any substitution. If he does make a substitution, both the animal and its substitute become holy and cannot be redeemed (Leviticus 27:30–33).

Passages like these are not talking about money but about tithes that the people were to give each year after they had finished harvesting their produce. Already in Leviticus 27, we see the principle of honoring the Lord "with your wealth, with the firstfruits of all your crops" (Proverbs 3:9). The people were asked to give God their first and best, rather than the leftovers or anything inferior. We ought to remember that God gave His one and only begotten Son as a sacrifice for our sins. For that reason, God deserves nothing less than the best from all of us.

There was a first tithe given to the Levites to support them and a second tithe to sponsor the religious festivals. The people were permitted to sell part of the tithe and bring the money to Jerusalem in order to purchase goods for the festival (Deuteronomy 14:22–29, Numbers 18:21, Nehemiah 12:44, Malachi 3:8–12). They left some of the tithe for the poor, the widows, and orphans.

Here are some important point to consider about tithing:

The tithe is the first 10 percent
"Be sure to set aside a tenth of all that your fields produce each year" (Deuteronomy 14:22). The children of Israel were asked to give 10 percent of their produce of the earth and the increase of their herds and flocks to God (Leviticus 27:30–34). The 10 percent was usually from the gross before any other expenses were made. It was not from the leftovers! Later on, when the priests started giving God their leftovers, God was not happy with them and told them, "A son honors his father, and a servant his master. If I am a father, where is the honor due me?" says the Lord Almighty. "It is you, O priests, who show contempt for my name" (Malachi 1:6).

Pushpay Blog, commenting on tithing, explained this further:

> Tithing wasn't something Israel did in the same way we mindlessly toss a gratuity down with our bill at a restaurant. It was an intentional practice that God used to teach Israel about his sovereign ownership of everything. Instead of being consumers of their blessings, they had to stop and think through just how much blessing they had.[3]

Jesus also addressed the giver's attitude when giving the tithe. Val Boyle wrote, "Jesus was rebuking the Scribes and Pharisees who were subject to the law and obligated to tithe anyway. The issue Jesus was addressing was not their tithes, but their neglect of justice, mercy and faithfulness toward others"[4] in Matthew 23:23.

Many believers want to know if contemporary Christians who are under grace are obligated today to tithe as Israel was commanded in the Old Testament. But there are no passages anywhere in the Scripture that mandate that Christians tithe as the Jewish people did. Christians are to give according to New Testament principles, which this book will take up later. If we understand New Testament teaching on giving correctly, it is actually good to give *more* than 10 percent of our income.

Tithe belongs to God

"A tithe of everything from the land, whether grain from the soil or fruit from the trees, belongs to the Lord; it is holy to the Lord" (Leviticus 27:30). One thing that we can learn from this passage is that when we give our money to the church or any Christian institution, we are giving it to God, and not to the pastor or the leaders of the organization. And when we fail to give as we should, we are robbing God (Malachi 3:8, see also Matthew 22:21). That is what happened with ancient Israel. Chris Cree wrote:

> God formally instituted the tithe in the Old Covenant Law of Moses. The tithe was to be offered to the priests and was to be used to support the priests and the Levites. And as with most of the Law, God's people weren't very good at keeping up with the tithe.[5]

The tithe is to be given in faith

"'I will prevent pests from devouring your crops, and the vines in your fields will not cast their fruit,' says the Lord Almighty" (Malachi 3:11). When we tithed in faith, our Lord promises to rebuke the devourer. That implies that God will protect us from problems and diseases. Believers are to tithe in faith and God will open the windows of heaven over their lives. "Without faith it is impossible to please Him" (Hebrews 11:6). Kenneth Copeland specifically comments on tithing by faith: "If you aren't tithing faithfully, your priorities are in the wrong place. Your priorities are in the natural realm instead of the spiritual realm. And it's what's in the spiritual realm that will bring you out of trouble and cause you to be abundantly blessed."[6]

Tithing 10 percent protects the other 90 percent

"I will rebuke the devourer for your sakes, and he shall not destroy the fruits of your ground" (Malachi 3:11 NASB). In commenting further on this passage, Kenneth Copeland encouraged the giver as follows:

> Give God what is His, and He will protect what is yours. As you honor God with the 10 percent that belongs to Him, He'll get involved with the rest. The other 90 percent will go further than ever before because you've got the supernatural power of God involved with your finances.[7]

God said, "Prove me" in tithing

God wants to bless us abundantly if we obey His commands. He wants us to test Him in giving our tithes and offerings, and He will bless us in a way that will overwhelm us. "'Bring the whole tithe into the storehouse, that there may be food in my house. Test me in this,' says the Lord Almighty, 'and see if I will not throw open the floodgates of heaven and pour out so much blessing that you will not have room enough for it'" (Malachi 3:10). As Jerry Savelle pointed out, "If you're not a sower [or a tither], you're not entitled to a harvest."[8]

Tithing is for our benefit

The following passage occurs in a context describing the joy those in the Old Testament receive when they give: "Then you…shall rejoice in all the good things the Lord your God has given to you and your household" (Deuteronomy 26:11). When we tithe, we are sowing a seed, and later we will reap the harvest of the seed we have sown. That is why the Scriptures tell us, "Honor the Lord with your wealth, with the first fruits of all your crops; then your barns will be filled to overflowing, and your vats will brim over with new wine" (Proverbs 3:9–10). Copeland confirms that when we give, we ourselves receive blessing: "God reinvests it back into our benefit. The tithe protects the harvest. You can't sow unless you're tithing— tithing comes first. The benefits are beyond anything you could ever imagine."[9]

Tithing was our covenant with God in the Old Testament
They have violated my covenant, which I commanded them to keep. They have taken some of the devoted things; they have stolen, they have lied, they have put them with their own possessions. That is why the Israelites cannot stand against their enemies. (Joshua 7: 11–12)

In the Old Testament, refusing to tithe disconnected someone from the covenant of blessing. When you gave in the Old Testament, God would bless you richly and defend you from destruction or evil. New Testament believers were never commanded to tithe. Second Corinthians 9:6–7 gives us guidelines for our giving to God and His work in this New Testament covenant: "But this I say: He who sows sparingly will also reap sparingly, and he who sows bountifully will also reap bountifully. So let each one give as he purposes in his heart, not grudgingly or of necessity; for God loves a cheerful giver."

Not tithing prevents your blessing from God
One of the ways the Israelites violated their covenant relationship with God was in not giving their tithes as He had commanded. God specifically reprimanded them for that:

> From the days of your fathers you have turned aside from my statutes and have not kept them. Return to me, and I will return to you, says the Lord of hosts. But you say, "How shall we return?"[8] Will man rob God? Yet you are robbing me. But you say, "How have we robbed you?" In your tithes and contributions.[9] You are cursed with a curse, for you are robbing me, the whole nation of you.[10] Bring the full tithe into the storehouse, that there may be food in my house. And thereby put me to the test, says the Lord of hosts, if I will not open the windows of heaven for you and pour down for you a blessing until there is no more need. (Malachi 3:7–10)

When we refuse to give to God, our blessings are also hindered. Although the tithe was an Old Testament covenant instruction, it is mentioned in the New Testament. Jesus corrected the religious leaders of His day, proclaiming to them, "Woe to you, teachers of the law and Pharisees, you hypocrites! You give a tenth of your spices — mint, dill and cumin. But you have neglected the more important matters of the law—justice, mercy and faithfulness. You should have practiced the latter, without neglecting the former" (Matthew 23:23, see also Luke 11:42). In one of Jesus's parables, the Pharisee in the temple prayed, "I fast twice a week; I pay tithes of all that I get" (Luke 18:12).

Yet for many reasons, not all of the details of the Old Testament Law are incumbent upon believers today. For example, Hebrews 7:1–10 shows that the priesthood of Jesus Christ has surpassed the Old Testament Levitical priesthood. Hebrews 9:6–26, 10:1–18 teaches us that the sacrifice of Jesus has surpassed and replaced all of the Old Testament sacrifices. The New Covenant that Jesus brought has made the Old Covenant *obsolete and outdated*, soon to *disappear* (Hebrews 10:13).

Although the Old Testament required tithing, it is never commanded in the New Testament; instead, believers are exhorted to follow the example of Christ in their giving. Anderson wrote, "The Scriptures do not teach that the tithe is incumbent upon New Testament believers. However, they teach that Christians are to be generous, sacrificial, expectant and cheerful givers!"[10] Val Boyles' comments on tithing is worthy of note here:

It needs to be re-stated that while there is extensive teaching on Christians giving to the work of God in the New Testament, there are no scriptures whatever that teach tithing. What they do teach is that Christians belong to God and what they have is held as a trust for him. Their giving is done to help those in need and to advance the Kingdom of God. They are only obliged to give in accordance with their means, out of what they have, and the amount they give is not as important as their willingness to give it. Giving is seen as proof of their love.[11]

Conclusion

The Lord God Almighty commanded the Israelites to give to Him in the form of the tithe or 10 percent. This was one way they were to respond to the many blessings He had given them. This tithe was the starting point. When you calculate all the tithes they were to give, it averaged out to about 23 percent a year. Blessings followed their obedience to God's command. When they disobeyed the command and withheld the tithes, He would allow the devourer to devour their money, produce, etc. (Malachi 3:8–11).

Giving to God is always voluntary, as opposed to giving to the government in taxes, which is compulsory. When we give, we are giving to God, out of what He has blessed us with. We should give willingly and by faith, believing that God will reward us for our cheerful giving.

Today, Christians can start with giving the 10 percent. But the New Testament concept of giving focuses more on our *attitude* in giving than on the amount. We are to give cheerfully, out of our own free will, generously, sacrificially, and purposefully, according to how God has blessed us as individuals. We are never to give grudgingly, or out of necessity. We will look at these principles of New Testament giving in the next chapters.

Reference for Chapter 1

2. Brian Anderson, Old Testament Tithing Vs. New
3. https://pushpay.com/blog/20-bible-verses-about.tithing/
4. Val Boyle https://bible-truths-revealed.com/adv15.html
5. Chris Cree, "2 Ways God Promises to Benefit You for Tithing" https://newcreeations.org/god-promises-benefits-tithing/?https://blog.kcm.org/tithing-101-the-10-bible-truths-you-need-to-know/?gclid=EAlalQobChMl2rfVfmJ7AlV7Vrx6tBh38ogx7EAMYASAEgL72vD BwE
6. Kenneth Copeland, Tithing 101: The Top 10 Bible Truths You Need to Know, https://blog.kcm.org/tithing-101-the-top-10-bible-truths-you-need-to-know/?
7. http:www.jerrysavelle.org
8. Kenneth Copeland, Tithing 101: The Top 10 Bible Truths You Need to Know,
9. https://blog.kcm.org/tithing-101-the-top-10-bible-truths-you-need-to-know/?
10. Brian Anderson, https://www.thebridgeonline.net/author/brian/
11. https://bible-truths-revealed.com/adv15.html

Chapter 2

The Motives and Purposes of Christian Giving

Before giving generously and sacrificially, a Christian needs to have the right motivation and purpose. Since all things we have come from God, we need to acknowledge the receipt of them. Believers should know that we are only stewards of whatever we supposedly *possess*. John MacArthur explained it this way:

> The first thing we learned in this series is that God does not need your money. He already owns everything. He is autonomous and self-sufficient and therefore does not need anything including you. The fact that He desires a relationship with you is simply the extension of His character of love and grace for your benefit. In addition, we also learned that all that you think you own belongs to God. You are a steward of what God has entrusted to you while you are here on this earth. You will not be taking any of it with you when you die. Since you are a steward, then you are responsible for what you have and will give account of your usage of it when you stand before God.[12]

God's Ownership of All Possessions
David says, "The earth is the Lord's, and everything in it, the world, and all who live in it" (Psalm 24:1). In one of the Psalms of Asaph,

the Lord tells us, "Every beast of the forest is mine, the cattle on a thousand hills. I know every bird of the mountains, and everything that moves in the field is mine. If I were hungry, I would not tell you, for the world is mine and all it contains" (Psalm 50:10–12 NASB). We are only stewards, taking care of all that God has given unto us. We are accountable to the things God has entrusted into our care. Giving is a natural way for us to express our thankfulness to God.

Realizing that it is more blessed to give than to receive should motivate us to give. It is not good to attack the church for being a money-raising machine unless one is ready to set an example of free, voluntary, and generous giving.[13]

The nature of God and our relationship with Him should influence how we give. John 3:16 informs us that "God so loved the world that He gave His one and only Son." God gave us the perfect example of how to put love into action. He gave because of the love He has for humankind; His love should motivate us to give as well. God is love, so we should imitate God's love (1 John 3:16–18, 4:10–11). The quality of our giving, therefore, can be measured by the motives for which the gift is given and the intended result or outcome. But there are right and wrong motives of giving.

Right Motives for Christian Giving

There are many excellent motives for giving to God because we want to glorify Him, because we belong to Him, because we have received so much from Him, because our gift matters to God, and many others. In this section, we are going to focus on five motives that the Scripture give special attention to.

To imitate Christ

Jesus gave Himself, and an excellent motive for us to give is to imitate Jesus. Although Jesus is God, He became man to redeem us. It is hard to grasp just how much Jesus gave up. The Bible says that "all things were created by Him and for Him" (Colossians 1:16). Christ was rich because He made all things, "yet for your sakes he became poor, so that you through his poverty might become rich" (2 Corinthians 8:9). He veiled the Godhead in humanity; when He became man, His divine power was restricted. He gave Himself voluntarily (John 10:15, 18) because love, compassion, and affection compelled Him to do so (Philippians 2:5–11).

The purpose of this act was for man's enrichment. Mankind was poor, lost, broken, and condemned, but through Christ's poverty, we can gain forgiveness, salvation, new life, holiness, and so much more. We can even "participate in the divine nature" (2 Peter 1:4). Since Christ did so much for us, we should try all that lies within our power to do similar things for our neighbors or for our church.[14] The love of Christ should constrain us to love Him, His people, and His work, to the extent of using our possessions for whatever ministry He has called us to.

Isaac Watts, realizing this great work of Christ for humanity, expressed the idea in his hymn, "When I Survey the Wondrous Cross": See, from His head, His hands, His feet, Sorrow and love flow mingled down, Did e'er such love and sorrow meet, Or thorn compose so rich a crown? Were the whole realm of nature mine, That were a present far too small, Love so amazing, so divine, Demands my soul, my life, my all.[15]

Brian Anderson, writing on the motivation for our giving, explained it this way:

> As those who believe on Him, we have inherited great riches: forgiveness, adoption, justification, the indwelling Spirit, peace with God, access to God, sanctification, and eternal glory to come! Notice that Christ didn't just give ten percent of His resources to obtain these spiritual treasures for us! He didn't even give fifty percent! He gave 100 percent! A disciple naturally desires to be like his master. Therefore, let us strive to emulate

our Lord. Let us not be content with giving a small fraction of our income, but pray that God would enable us to give more and more to help hurting people and expand the kingdom of God around the world![16]

To prove the reality of one's love

The proof of one's love is often expressed in giving. One person may show love towards God by dedicating one's life to Him. Another may show love for people by helping those who are having problems (1 John 3:17). If we love the church and all its works, we should give for the welfare of the church. If we love our neighbors, we should give our time and money to alleviate their problems. God's love for humankind compelled Him to give His Son, Jesus Christ (John 3:16). The love of Christ caused Him to give His life to the extent of dying on the cross to deliver us from our sins. When Christ said, "Render to Caesar the things that are Caesar's and to God the things that are God's" (Matthew 22:21), He showed that giving to God is just as essential a proof of love for Him as the payment of taxes is a proof of loyalty to one's state or country.

It was love that compelled the Macedonian Christians to give sacrificially to the suffering Christians in Jerusalem, in spite of their own afflictions and poverty (2 Corinthians 8:1–4). Hattie Bell Allen stated the idea beautifully:

> The love of Christ constrains us to give everything. You think of all that Jesus did for you in dying to save you; do you not want to do all you can to help all the people of all the world to know him, too, and be saved, as you are?[17]

Giving in some ways proves our love more conclusively than depth of knowledge, length of prayers, or prominence of service.[18] "The glory of giving is in the quality of love, and it never fails to find something to bestow."[19]

To help meet the needs of others

Scripture is replete with encouragements to give materially and to help those in need. In Old Testament times, the Israelites were required to share what they had with the fatherless, widows, and the poor during festivals (Deuteronomy 16:1–12) and at other times (Leviticus 19:9–10). In the time of the apostles, most people were poor, and the gap between the rich and the poor was very great. This is still very true in many parts of the world today, including Nigeria. The Jerusalem church was a well-known example in giving to assist the poor (Acts 2:44–45; 4:34–35; 6:1). Later famine relief money was sent by the Christians in Antioch to those in Judea: "Then the disciples, every man according to his ability, determined to send relief unto the brethren which dwelt in Judea, which also they did, and sent it to the elders by the hands of Barnabas and Saul" (Acts 11:29–30). Paul praised the churches of Macedonia and Achaia for giving to the poor saints in Jerusalem (Romans 15:25–27).

To give to one's family is an obligation for all Christians alike. As the Bible teaches, "If anyone does not provide for his relatives, and especially for his immediate family, he has denied the faith and is worse than an unbeliever" (1 Timothy 5:8). This is particularly important due to the extended family system in Nigeria. There your in-laws, cousins, nephews, nieces, brothers, sisters, and, of course, father and mother are to be taken care of no matter what your financial situation may be.

But in the family of God, we need to meet the needs of other Christians as well. Dr. Charles C. Ryrie even goes so far as to say that "our primary responsibility in the use of money is to care for the material needs of other believers" (Galatians 6:10).[20] Christians ought to show empathy with the suffering masses around them, to the extent of giving to alleviate their problems. "Giving to refugees and starving people in other lands, the victims of war, earthquake and other disasters and those in other lands who suffer from injustice like in Africa is commendable."[21]

Christians need to give in support of the widows, orphans, and the needy. Allen brought this point home quite effectively:

> Your money may stand for you as you help to support the orphans and the helpless ones and the work of hospitals. Your gifts mean more, don't they, when you think of them as going where you cannot go and serving where you cannot serve?[22]

Many Christians know the story of a certain rich young man who came to Jesus to inquire what he must do to inherit eternal life. Jesus first directed him toward the commandments: Do not kill; do not commit adultery; do not steal; do not bear false witness; honor your father and your mother. This young man answered immediately, "All these I have kept since I was a boy" (Mark 10:20).[23] Jesus looked at him and loved him, knowing that the man was correct in his statement.

"'One thing you lack,' he said. 'Go, sell everything you have and give to the poor, and you will have treasure in heaven. Then come, follow me'" (Mark 10:21). The man grieved at the statement of Jesus because he had great possessions. He went away sorrowful but did not come back to Jesus. Jesus commented, "How hard it is for the rich to enter the kingdom of God" (Mark 10:23). Jesus wasn't condemning having money, He wanted to show the mistake of putting money before God, as well as the importance of helping the needy (see also Matthew 25:37–40).

Jesus told his disciples, "Sell your possessions and give to the poor. Provide purses for yourselves that will not wear out, a treasure in heaven that will not be exhausted, where no thief comes near and no moth destroys. For where your treasure is, there your heart will be also" (Luke 12:33–34, see also Ephesians 4:28, James 1:27). This passage advises us to support the underprivileged people in our midst: the orphans, widows, and those in need. We are to give out of our love for others and our love for Jesus. We are not to announce our gifts to people in order to receive their praise. It is to be done in secret "so the Lord that sees in secret will reward us for the good deeds that we have done" (Matthew 6:1–4).

To support minsters and the gospel
"The elders who direct the affairs of the church are worthy of double honor, especially those whose work is preaching and teaching the gospel. For the Scripture says, 'Do not muzzle the ox while it is treading out grain,' and 'The worker deserves his wages'" (1 Timothy 5:17–18). Many people whom God has called to the ministry have been hindered from being trained in seminaries and Bible colleges due to lack of finances. This is also true of other people who are not privileged to attend other institutions of higher learning or receive training for a trade. This problem is very prevalent in African countries and other places in the world where you have to pay for most of your education from kindergarten to the university level.

This neglect of God's servants also applies to paying pastors in the church. S. A. Aluko addresses the issue very directly when he write, "We Christians hold our services in churches and go home to rest, leaving it only to the clergy to carry on church administration and evangelizing. We do not believe in sacrificing time and money for the propagation of our faith."[24] Aluko later adds this scorching rebuke:

> The present (payment of) the ministers of religion is sadly low. It drives away many vital, brilliant and religious people from the ministry. It reduces the attraction and the influence of Christianity in our society. The Christian profession has now to compete with the other professions for the best men in our society, if the church is to retain its position of preeminence. We must reexamine our attitude to this problem and see that the due and fitting training and payment of church workers comes

before everything, including before our church educational programs.[25]

The work of winning the world cannot be carried out without trained leadership. The Christian "widow's mite" can help to train students in both our seminaries and Bible colleges and, in this way, produce those who will be our future Christian leaders.

The support from Christians would help to send out pastors and missionaries to the hinterlands of the world for the spreading of the Gospel of Christ. Allen's comments on this topic are most inspiring:

> You help to pay the pastor for his loyal services and in supporting him you are preaching through him. You help to provide literature for all the organizations of the church. Your gifts help to keep the church building in good condition, provide for music, lighting, and other necessary things, thus contributing to worship, study and training.[26]

Charles C. Ryrie, commenting on the issue of supporting missionary workers, points out, "Paul and his associates were helped in their missionary work. The Philippian church gave to Paul on at least three occasions (Philippian 4:16), and Paul rigorously defended the right of those engaged in the work to be supported by others."[27]

The Apostle Paul, writing to the Corinthians, very directly encouraged them to support Christian workers financially: "In the same way, the Lord has commanded that those who preach the gospel should receive their living from the gospel" (1 Corinthians 9:14). Not only should Christians give in support of pastors but also others who labor for the Lord as well. As Anderson put it:

> Here we have the testimony of Scripture that God approves when we use money to support faithful Christian workers. Therefore,

it is important that God's people utilize their financial resources to support other Christian workers, whether they be elders of a local church, or itinerant evangelists, or missionaries.[28]

To receive God's blessings and rewards

God does bless his children in several ways, just as He has promised (Malachi 3:10). The principle that "whoever sows sparingly will also reap sparingly, and whoever sows generously will also reap generously" (2 Corinthians 9:6) is born out in both the New and Old Testaments. When Paul commended the Philippian church for their generosity toward his ministry, he spoke of more being credited to their *account* (Philippians 4:17). This implies that God will give more blessings to those who give abundantly. Generous gifts inspire in the recipients, many prayers, and intercessions on behalf of the giver: "They long for you and pray for you" (2 Corinthians 9:14). The giver gives his money while the receiver gives his prayers in exchange; such prayers can move the hand of God for blessings which the physical money cannot produce.[29] Jesus taught that a generous-hearted person and faithful giver will be rewarded with kind treatment by his fellowmen: "Do not judge, and you will not be judged. Do not condemn, and you will not be condemned. Forgive, and you will be forgiven. Give, and it will be given to you. A good measure, pressed down, shaken together and running over, will be poured into your lap. For with the measure you use, it will be measured to you" (Luke 6:37–38).

When the people of Judah revived giving to the Lord in the days of King Hezekiah, they themselves received from Him in abundance: "Since the people began to bring the offerings into the house of the Lord, we have had enough to eat, and have left plenty: for the Lord hath blessed his people; and that which is left is this great store" (2 Chronicles 31:10). God often bestows material prosperity to his faithful children. The secret of prosperity and of success which he gave Joshua was based solely on his dedication (Joshua 1:7–8). The rewards of godly giving are that

God will enable you to give even more. Thanksgiving will be made to God. God will be glorified because of you. And people will pray for you.

Many things will happen when believers give with a right motive. God will meet our needs (Philippians 4:17–19). The needs of the poor will be met (Philippians 4:16, 18; 2 Corinthians 8:13–14; 9:12). God will be thanked and glorified (2 Corinthians 9:11–13, 15). The body of Christ would be unified in prayer and fellowship (2 Corinthians 9:14). And people will spend eternity with God because of your giving.[30]

Having dealt with the right motives for giving, it is expedient that we recognize the *wrong* motives for giving as well.

Wrong Motives of Giving
When your motivation for giving is to twist God's arms or manipulate Him to gain favor in return, you are misguided by your selfishness and lack of understanding. Lugt and Smith's observation about *maintaining* the right intentions in giving materially and receiving blessing is right on point: "Faithfulness and generosity in giving brings rewards, but the motive for giving must never be selfish desire for financial return or a feeling that contribution will manipulate God into doing something for you."[31] No one can bribe God with gifts because acceptance of bribery is not consistent with His nature.

Giving is from the heart, and it has to come from a grateful one. Anytime anybody decides to give gifts to help people, church, or missions, it should be done with right motive, not for self-elevation or showing of wealth. For example, Jesus condemned the Pharisees for their arrogance when they gave (Matthew 23:23–24).

There is a saying that good living produces good giving, while bad living produces bad giving. Many people in the Bible serve as examples of that principle. What do we think about the offerings of Cain and Abel? Is it not the bad attitude of covetousness that led Cain to offer an unacceptable offering to God? His brother Abel gave bountifully out of a good heart. What about Saul? Was not his bad giving condemned by Samuel? "Does the Lord delight in burnt offerings and sacrifices, as much as in obeying the Lord? To obey is better than sacrifice, and to heed is better than the fat of rams" (1 Samuel 15:22). Were not the gifts of the wicked Israelites of Isaiah's day rejected (Isaiah 1:13)? What about the evil priests of Hosea's day (Hosea 6:4–6)? Were not the evil gifts of the Pharisees rejected (Matthew 23:23–24)? A candid answer to each of these questions should influence the Christians to examine the way and manner he or she should give his gifts.

To exalt oneself (pride)
Command those who are rich in this present world not to be arrogant nor to put their hope in wealth, which is so uncertain, but to put their hope in God, who richly provides us with everything for our enjoyment. Command them to do good, to be rich in good deeds, and to be generous and willing to share. In this way they will lay up treasure for themselves as a firm foundation for the coming age, so that they may take hold of the life that is truly life. (1 Timothy 6:17–19)

Paul's exhortation to Timothy to charge those who are rich *not to be arrogant* should be uppermost in the heart of every Christian. Many people today give their gifts in order to exalt themselves even in our churches. They announce their gift so that people will praise them for giving a fabulous amount. They overlook Christ's warning concerning such an approach to giving (Matthew 6:1–4).[32] Lugt and Smith illustrate this unscriptural attitude with this modern example: "A business man who gives $20 every week once thought, 'The pastor and deacons better be thankful that I'm here to do this. They'd miss my money if I ever decided to go to another church.'"[33]

The fact is that nothing we do for God has any value in His sight unless it expresses gratitude, love, faith, and a desire to do His will. And that includes giving! As long as a person is proud of his abilities and accomplishments and tries to enhance his own reputation by his giving, he is a reproach to the Lord. As long as a haughty attitude prevails, our giving, however generous it may appear, is an abomination in the sight of the Almighty God. As Steven J. Cole wrote, "If you give to be honored by men for your great generosity, you are giving for the wrong reason. Giving is to be done in secret before God" (Matthew 6:1–4).

To gain favor from God and man

Another wrong motive is to gain favor. The belief that the money Christians cast in the offering plate earned them favor with God or obligates God to them, is very wrong. Jesus spoke about the meticulous nature of the Pharisees in their giving. They relied on their giving as a way of gaining favor in the sight of God (Matthew 23:23–24). They were synagogue-attending, praying, tithing people, but they hated and crucified the Savior. So mere outward service, whether with money or any other form or ceremony, does not satisfy God's demands.[34] He wanted us to be holy (Matthew 5:20).

Any Christian who thinks that giving dollars and cents can gain God's favor is making a mistake. One may succeed in gaining man's favor because of the money one give, but it does not impress God. If we give to be applauded by men, we have received our due reward here on earth (Matthew 6:1–4). David once said, "The sacrifices of God are a broken spirit; a broken and contrite heart, O God, you will not despise" (Psalm 51:17). Steve J. Cole commented:

> Money is power. Some people threaten to take their large gifts elsewhere if you don't do what they want. That may be how politics operates, but that isn't how God's church operates. It's wrong to show preference to the wealthy (James 2:1–9). It's sin to use your money to try to buy spiritual influence (Acts 8:9–24).[35]

To give out of guilt

We should not give because we feel guilty about having so much wealth. It is great to be good stewards of what God has blessed us with. We shouldn't be pressured to give. We have received freely, and we should give freely, not out of compulsion.

To receive reward in return

The next wrong motive of giving is expecting to receive a reward in return. Among those who have such motives, they think that their receiving depends on their giving. They think it is a bargain and that either God or man is obligated in giving them back; hence, they have given. Bishop Azariah put it this way: "They have thought of giving as a bargain. If I give you, you will in turn give me. If I give God, He will give me."[36]

To respond to gimmicks

Many people are pressured into giving by televangelists and telemarketers. Some of the things they say include:

> "For your donation, I'll send you my latest book." "The names of my loved ones will be entered in a special book to be placed in the lobby of the new building." Or the worst is, "We'll send you a special prayer cloth, blessed by brother so-and-so." These are all worldly gimmicks, opposed to the biblical giving.[37]

It is odd to think of giving as an investment and feel that God is forced to grant you a good return. The Bible advises us to give in a way so that we will not expect the people whom we have given to give us back in return (Luke 6:34–35). If our giving depends on what we will receive in return, we are no better than the Pharisees. Dr. Ryrie once wrote, "Material blessing is never promised today as an automatic reward for faithfulness in any area of Christian living including giving."[38] It is better to give simply, without ulterior motives. That is the way God gives to his children, and that is the pattern that God wants us to follow (James 1:5, Romans 12:8). As Lugt and Smith put it, "Giving because you figure you're going to get it back is like being good to an old person because you want to be included in his will."[39]

Conclusion

There are definitely right and wrong motives of Christian giving. I strongly believe that mankind's possessions are all from God. We are all stewards of what God has given to us. The right motives of Christian giving include imitating Christ in giving. Christ gave Himself in order to redeem humankind from all of our sins. Our giving should aim at alleviating the sufferings of people.

Giving is a proof of one's love (1 John 3:16–18). It should be for us a way of imitating Christ. It should prove the reality of our love. It should aim at helping those who are in need. And of course, giving should be supporting ministers, missionaries, and missions. When we give, we open the door to receive God's blessings and rewards ourselves.

But giving that exalts oneself, seeks to gain God's favor, tries to impress man, or hopes specifically to secure a reward is very wrong and should be done away with.

Now that we have examined our motives for giving, we are ready to consider the principles and methods of Christian giving.

Reference for Chapter 2

12. John MacArthur, "Principles of Godly Giving, Pt. 1–2 Corinthians 8 and 9," https:/gracebibleny.org/principles_of_godly_giving_pt_1_2_corinthians_8_9.
13. R. M. Burke, *Pounds and Pennies* (Ibadan, Nigeria: Daystar Press, 1967), p. 11.
14. H. D. M. Spence, Joseph S. Exell, *The Pulpit Commentary on Corinthians*, Vol. 19 (Grand Rapids, Michigan: Eerdmans Publishing Company, 1962), p. 208.
15. Ira D. Sankey, *Sacred Songs and Solos* (London: Marshall Morgan and Scott, n.d.), p. 115.
16. Brian Anderson, https:/w.thebridgeonline.net/author/brian/
17. Hattie Bell Allen, *Living for Jesus* (Nashville, Tennessee: The Sunday School Board of the Southern Baptist Convention, 1939), p. 81.
18. Dr. Charles Caldwell Ryrie, *Balancing the Christian Life* (Chicago: Moody Press, 1981), p. 84.
19. Spence, p. 201.
20. Dr. Charles Caldwell Ryrie, *What You Should Know About Responsibility* (Chicago: Moody Press, 1982), p. 91.
21. Burke, p. 12.
22. Allen, p. 83.
23. S. A. Aluko, *Christianity and Communism* (Ibadan, Nigeria: Daystar Press, 1964), p. 56.
24. Aluko, p. 56.
25. Aluko, p. 69.
26. Allen, p. 83.
27. Ryrie, *Social Responsibility*, p. 92.
28. Anderson, https://www.thebridgeonline.net/author/brian/
29. V. S. Azariah, *Christian Giving* (New York, New York: World Christian Boks Association Pres, 195), p. 74.
30. https://bible.org/seriespag/lesson-5-giving-god-s-way-selected-scriptures

31. Vander H. Lugt and Carl H. Smith, *As Usher Come Forward. Grand Rapids* (Michigan: Radio Bible, 1976), p. 61
32. Lugt and Smith, p. 19.
33. Ibid, p. 19.
34. John R. Rice, *All About Christian Giving* (Wheaton, Illinois: Sword of the Lord Publishers, 1954), p. 12.
35. https://bible.org/seriespage/lesson-5-giving-god-s-way-selected-scriptures
36. Bishop Azariah, p. 87.
37. https://bible.org/seriespage/lesson-5-giving-god-s-way-selected-scriptures
38. Ryrie, *Christian Life*, p. 88.
39. Lugt and Smith, p. 55.

Chapter 3

The Principles and Methods of Christian Giving

The subject of Christian giving is not a burdensome one, weighing the believer heavily with responsibility as many people think; it is rather a very happy one. Giving to Jesus Christ, giving to get out the blessed gospel, giving to people material things, and giving to those who have blessed us with spiritual things, is one of the greatest privileges and joys of a Christian. You will see this as we consider the biblical principles and methods of giving.

The Principles of Christian Giving
Christian giving is a grace, a gift of God, which is made possible through the enablement of the Holy Spirit. It is an evidence of God's gracious work in the hearts of believing men and women. As such, it is in contrast to the principle of law, which imposes giving as a compulsory requirement. Christian giving is characterized by the following principles.

Giving out of joy
The Macedonian Christians who were under affliction and poverty learned the importance of giving with *overwhelming joy*, both to the Lord and to their brothers and sisters in the Lord (2 Corinthians 8:2). This ought to be the principle that guides Christian giving. It, therefore, emphasizes that giving should never be "reluctantly or under compulsion" (2 Corinthians 9:7). Giving is to be joyous and generous.

We are to share with other less fortunate than we are, and to give unselfishly without anticipating something in return (Luke 14:13–14).[40]

Giving despite affliction

Giving should not only be joyous, it should be done when one is afflicted. And now, brothers and sisters, we want you to know about the grace that God has given the Macedonian churches. In the midst of a very severe trial, their overflowing joy and their extreme poverty welled up in rich generosity. For I testify that they gave as much as they were able, and even beyond their ability. Entirely on their own, they urgently pleaded with us for the privilege of sharing in this service to the Lord's people. And they exceeded our expectations: They gave themselves first of all to the Lord, and then by the will of God also to us. (2 Corinthians 8:1–5)

Paul set the Macedonian Christians as an example to the Corinthian Christians, in order to stimulate them to give in the right way. The persecution and tribulation caused by the Macedonian's non-Christian countrymen never stopped them from giving to God and His ministry. Today's Christian should consider the Macedonian example as well and give like they did. Bishop Azariah wrote:

> If we are fully dedicated to God, the fact of distress, persecution, and affliction, and the consequent life of constant dread and anxiety, will not interfere with the relationship of our Christians to God, and to giving.[41]

Giving despite poverty

As affliction was no obstacle to giving, so poverty should not be a hindrance either. Although many Christians in the New Testament world struggled with finances, their giving was not hindered by poverty. As it was then, it was often true now "the Christians who have the least to give, who struggle to make ends meet, often are the ones who surprise us most with their sacrificial giving. And at the same time, it is often those who have an abundance that are stingy and grudging. Money tends to harden the heart. It dries up the wells of sympathy in some people."[42]

Jesus Himself showed us that poverty does not prevent sacrificial giving, when He cited the example of the poor widow:

> As Jesus looked up, he saw the rich putting their gifts into the temple treasury. He also saw a poor widow put in two very small copper coins. "Truly I tell you," he said, "this poor widow has put in more than all the others. All these people gave their gifts out of their wealth; but she out of her poverty put in all she had to live on." (Luke 21:1–4)

Brian Anderson's encouragement to the poor is cited below:

> Moreover, those who have should not feel guilty if they are not able to give ten percent of their income. It is true that God will honor and bless the man who gives sacrificially. But believers must be given the freedom to give whatever they have purposed in their heart, without fear that others will judge them.[43]

The fact that poverty is not a barrier to generous giving led directly to the next principle that each should give according to his or her ability.

Giving according to one's ability
Giving in the Macedonian Church was according to each member's individual ability. An amount was not stipulated as it was in the Old Testament, which mandated 23 percent of one's income. A Christian should give according to how the Lord has prospered: "Each one of you should set aside a sum of money in keeping with your income" (1 Corinthians 16:2). Mr. A should not wait on Mr. B to give, before he gives his gift. He should not compare his gift with the other person's; he should give to the Lord according to what he himself is able to give.

The bad example of Ananias and Sapphira in giving (Acts 5:1–11) should not be copied but that of the poor widow should be upheld. The widow's gift was commended because of the heart with which she gave and the way she gave all she had. She even gave beyond her ability. Note how Jesus cared about the heart that gave and the sacrifice she made and not about the amount. "Our giving must be measured by what we have. A man's responsibility to contribute is not measured by some other's man ability to give, but by his own."[44]

Giving of oneself
Liberality springs from the surrendering of ourselves to the Lord, so that all we have, including our money, is at God's disposal. The Macedonians Christians gave not only their money, but *they gave themselves* also (2 Corinthians 8:5). Most Christians have indeed given much of themselves to the Lord. But they have failed to accomplish the monetary side of it. "Stinginess in the face of human needs is the system of an incompletely surrendered life."[45] It was the problem of greed which Jesus saw in the Pharisees that prompted His injunction to *seek first his kingdom and his righteousness, and these (material) things shall be given to you as well* (Matthew 6:33, see also 5:20, 6:24–32; Luke 16:14).

I was a full-time teacher until 2001. But because of our ministry, my wife and I decided that I should become a substitute teacher so that I could have more time to go to the mission field and spend as much time as possible in ministry. In order words, I became a *tentmaker*, using secular work to support my involvement in ministry like the apostle Paul did. My wife also was a full-time teacher, but she had to take an early retirement in 2011 in order to devote more time to the ministry.

There is no amount of money or time spent in God's work that is too much to give. Francis R. Havergal, who wrote the hymn "Take My Life and Let It Be" realized the essence of giving oneself:

Take my voice and let me sing Always, only, for my King; Take my lips, and let them be Filled with messages for thee. Take my silver and my gold, Not a mite would I withhold.

> Take my intellect, and use Every power as thou shalt choose. Take my love: my Lord, I pour At thy feet its treasure store. Take myself, and I will be Ever, only, All for Thee.

A successful giving habit erupts from a life dedicated and surrendered to God. "You see, the real thing that pleases God always in this matter of giving is that people should give themselves, their love, their devotion, their trust, their service, and all they have."[46] The Focus on the Family website encourages us to "give your appointments and plans to God first thing each day. Ask Him to show you how He wants you to use your time, talents, and resources, and give Him permission to interrupt your agenda."[47]

Giving eagerly, requesting the opportunity to give
The Macedonian Christians went as far as begging for an opportunity to give; so should we (2 Corinthians 8:4). It is nothing other than love that constrained them to beg for an opportunity to give their widow's mite to alleviate the suffering of the saints in Jerusalem. Clearly the example of the earliest church (Acts 2:44–45, 4:32–35) was strong in the minds of the Macedonians; hence, they believed in sharing what they had with those in need. No doubt they realized Christ's statement that "it is more blessed to give than to receive" (Acts 20:35).

But it is hard for the present-day Christians to beg for an opportunity to give. This is because of the desire to acquire as much wealth like the unbelievers around us. It is this writer's opinion that believers today, like the Macedonians of old, should seek for opportunities to express their Christian love through giving. "Giving to them was a privilege, a gain, not a loss."[48]

Giving of one's own accord

The giving that is not compelled is far better than giving that has been forced. When the children of Israel in the wilderness gave toward the building of the tabernacle, it was voluntary. The people gave as much or as little as they wished, and they gave more than what was needed. Moses had to command them not to bring further gifts for the work at hand (Exodus 35:4–9, 36:5–7).

Giving should not be out of compulsion for if it is, there will be no joy in such a giving. Some churches use techniques that are not scriptural to pressure members to give: high pressure fundraisers, quotas, checking pay stubs, assessments, harvest and building levies, class fees, bazaars, Annual Missionary Collection (AMC), and other methods. Some of these you may recognize as Western methods, some are African, but they are all contrary to the biblical principle of giving "what you have decided in your heart to give, not reluctantly or under compulsion" (2 Corinthians 9:7). People should be taught how they should give and why they should give. The needs of the church and of the individuals in the congregation should be made known to the members. They should be allowed to give of their own accord, willingly and voluntarily.[49] The New Testament passages on giving according to one's own decision include 2 Corinthians 8:3–4, 9, 9:7; 1 Timothy 6:18–19.

John Wesley's maxim to "earn all you can, save all you can, and give all can" should challenge every Christian.[50] Anderson points out that the biblical pattern for giving on one's accord goes back to the time before Moses: "This voluntary giving is exactly what Abraham and Jacob were doing before the institution of the law, and is what all Christians are to be doing today. Believers today are free to give the amount they choose to give." This type of giving shows our diligence to God's injunction. Rice wrote:

> How blessed it is when Christian people, not because the preacher is concerned, not because of the missionary pleas, but

because in their own loving hearts they long to give, they enjoy giving, and with their own holy devotion and zeal they bring their gifts.[51]

Believers should give because they have been given everything they possess. There shouldn't be any comparison of your gift with what other people have given to God. To put it another way, don't compete with people in their giving. Steve Diggs wrote:

> Each Christian's giving is a very personal experience, based on his or her financial ability. From the earliest days, God has made allowances for the financial disparity between His people. In Old Testament days, the better-heeled Jews were expected to bring a sacrificial lamb, while poorer followers were permitted to bring less expensive doves and pigeons.[52]

Giving generously

It is one thing to give of one's accord and another to give generously. The generosity of the early Christians under the compulsion of love far surpassed anything known among the Jewish people under the compulsion of law. The account of Luke in the Acts of the Apostles shows that they had all things in common, sold their possessions and goods, and distributed them as every person had need (Acts 2:44–45, 4:32–35).[53] The example of Barnabas is worthy of special note in this aspect of generosity (Acts 4:36–37).

Giving will not be generous, spontaneous, and joyful until it is regarded not as duty but as a privilege. This can happen only when we are concerned more about the needs of others than about our own needs and wants. Such care is the outstanding fruit of the Christian spirit. Charles C. Ryrie in his study Bible states that, "God will supply the generous giver with enough to meet his own needs and enough to give for every good deed."[54]

The great passage on giving in 2 Corinthians 8–9 compares giving to the act of sowing seed. "Remember this: Whoever sows sparingly will also reap sparingly, and whoever sows generously will also reap generously" (2 Corinthians 9:6). In the same manner, a Christian who gives sparingly to the Lord will in turn reap a meager blessing, while he who gives bountifully will reap bountifully.

It is better to lay up our treasure in heaven rather than on earth (Matthew 6:19–21). The Christian could do this effectively by investing his or her treasure in winning and nurturing eternal souls, either by supporting the church or giving to individuals who are in need. Oswald Smith explains the principle this way:

> You give to God in days of prosperity and God will give to you in days of depression. You withhold from God in days of prosperity and God will withhold from you in days of depression. If you faithfully give to God you will never find yourself in the breadline.[55]

Giving cheerfully

Paul's exhortation to the Corinthian Christians on giving cheerfully is great advice for all Christians: "Let each one do just as he has purposed in his heart; not grudgingly or under compulsion; for God loves a cheerful giver" (2 Corinthians 9:7). The idea of giving cheerfully could be explained as giving to cheer up those who are in need and giving it with an expression of joy on the face and in the heart.

In many countries of the world, in particular the so-called third world countries, churches employ levies as a way of grabbing money from their members. But if a church forces the people to give, they will not do so cheerfully.

Cheerful givers are objects of God's love. God does not care for our gifts if they are given grudgingly. Despite your poverty, give cheerfully as the

The Joy of Faithful and Cheerful Giving

Lord has prospered you, just as the poor widow in Mark 12 gave to the Lord, and she was commended.[56]

"Giving ought to be seen as a great privilege, not as a heavy burden or fearless duty. God doesn't want His people to give out of sense of compulsion, but rather from an attitude of joy and cheerfulness."[57]

Giving regularly

Paul's directions to the Corinthian Christians include setting aside money each week to give to the Lord's work: "On the first day of every week, each one of you should set aside a sum of money in keeping with your income, saving it up, so that when I come no collections will have to be made" (1 Corinthians 16:2). The regularity is obvious in the phrase, "On the first day of every week." This meant that the act of giving will be a continual one.

In their assembly or fellowship every Sunday, the early church practiced five main things: worship, instruction, fellowship, evangelism, and service (wives). The *service* included sharing their possessions with one another. The account of Acts 2:42–47 explicitly describes how giving material things to meet one another's needs was part of the ongoing worship life of the early Christians.

Paul's command regarding *the first day of every* week" is reflected in the common practice today of including a time of giving in the Sunday worship service. Charles Ryrie commenting on this even goes so far as to say that "the Lord's Day is God appointed for keeping accounts, determining proportions, and laying by in store."[58]

It is a command of God to give, and we are encouraged to do it regularly. As Allen put it, "Every Sunday bring your own offering, as much as you are able, to the Lord's house with joy in your heart."[59]

Giving proportionately

Christians are expected not only to give regularly, but they should give proportionately as well. Jesus gives the general idea when He says that "from everyone who has been given much, much will be demanded; and from the one who has been entrusted with much, much more will be asked" (Luke 12:48). This principle applies to many aspects of the Christian life, but the following passage applies it specifically to our giving: "Each one of you should set aside a sum of money in keeping with your income" (1 Corinthians 16:2).

What is meant by *proportionate giving*? If a Christian is earning about $300 a week, his giving would center around that income, while if another is earning about $1,000 a week, one would normally expect the second person to give more than the first, in proportion to his income. That is to say, if you receive more, you give more; if you receive less, you give less. But remember the Macedonians who gave *beyond* their ability (2 Corinthians 8:3).[60]

Giving sacrificially
"Sacrifice means the giving up of something of great value to oneself for a special purpose, or to benefit somebody else."[61] The Bible commends Christian giving that is sacrificial.
The poor widow in Luke 21:1–4 who gave all she had is a good example of sacrificial giving. It is not the amount she gave that won her the reputation of giving more than those who gave their gifts on that day. It is the amount left behind *after* giving, and the heart with which she gave, that have immortalized her. Many people today who express their giving as their widow's mite, do so wrongly. Let's say a man ha $1,000, and he gave $10 in an offering plate. What remains is $990. This amount that was given is not proportionate to the remainder and cannot be termed a sacrificial gift. It will be sacrificial when it is proportionate to the remainder, or beyond what is proportionate.

Giving sacrificially does not mean giving all we have, but giving ourselves, giving from our hearts, and giving even beyond what we might normally be expected to give. Giving sacrificially should lead one to a frugal life in order to support God's Kingdom work.

What I mean, brothers and sisters, is that time is short. From now on, those who have wives should live as if they do not; those who mourn, as if they did not; those who are happy, as if they were not; those who buy something, as if it were not theirs to keep; [31] those who use the things of the world, as if not engrossed in them.
For this world in its present form is passing away. (1 Corinthians 7:29–31)

Anderson challenges each one of us along these lines:

> Can you say that your own giving is characterized by a sacrificial spirit? Does your giving really cost you anything? It's not really how much we give that is so important, but how much we keep for ourselves after we've given. May our great and glorious God enable us to practice a joyful, sacrificial lifestyle of giving.

Giving should be sacrificial and should be practiced by every Christian. Soroki's comments on sacrificial giving make good food for thought for all of us:

> We should give sacrificially as we feel led by God and allow Him to use our giving to bring about a great harvest in the lives of others and in His church. The pattern of Christian giving is not box-checking and obligations. It is a daily lifestyle of kindness and generosity flowing from the Spirit which dwells within us.[62]

Giving is a requirement for every Christian
Paul in 1 Corinthians 16:2 instructs that "each one of you should set aside a sum of money in keeping with his income." This suggests that it is the duty of every Christian to set aside an amount. He did not say to let *some* Christians set aside their gifts. Thus, it is the obligation of every Christian to give no matter your financial situation.

If you are poor, you should give sacrificially, according to the example of the Macedonian Christians. If you are well-off, you are still enjoined to give according to the proportion of your earnings, bearing in mind that it is more blessed to give than to receive (Acts 20:35). As Ryrie puts it:

> Grace does not make giving optional; it is the privilege and responsibility of every Christian, and it is the concrete manifestation of his love of God. Giving is a personal matter in which every believer sustains a direct and individual responsibility to the Lord as if he were the only Christian in the world.[63]

Steven J. Cole, supporting the view that every Christian ought to give, has the following to add:

> Giving is for believers, and it should be done by all believers. Poor Christians as well as rich should give to the Lord (2 Corinthians 8:2, Luke 21:1–4). That is one reason it is wrong to be in debt because you aren't free to give generously when you owe creditors. But even if you can't give much, you aren't exempt from giving. Those who are supported in Christian ministry are not exempt either. In fact, they should set the example (Acts 20:35).[64]

It has become essential to emphasize the New Testament instructions on giving to present-day Christians. Misunderstandings about giving have come from bad examples and bad teaching, including the emphasis placed on the Old Testament system of tithing instead of the New Testament method of giving. But as Ryrie put it, "The Lord's work will never lack support if we preach and practice New Testament principles of giving."[65] The Focus on the Family website gives an excellent summary of how a Christian should approach finances and giving:

What does a good steward look like? We'd suggest that there are five key indicators of faithfulness with which he's carrying out his responsibilities. First, he gives generously in proportion with the level of his resources and abilities (2 Corinthians 8:12). Second, he exercises self-control by maintaining a debt-free lifestyle (Romans 13:8, Galatians 5:23). Third, he pays his taxes with integrity and an attitude of thanksgiving (Matthew 22:21, Romans 13:7). Fourth, he sets financial goals with an eye to the needs of the family and loved ones (1 Timothy 5:8). And fifth, he seeks the counsel of wise advisors and remains accountable to others in all his financial dealings (Proverbs 15:22).[66]

The Methods of Christian Giving

Having treated the principles that should guide our giving, it is expedient that we consider some of the methods Christians use as we give our gifts.

The New Testament commands giving of our resources, and gives several principles to follow as we give. However, each believer is given freedom as to *how* he or she gives, and what method of giving is to be employed. The Old Testament is full of practical ways of giving unto God, most of which seem to be out of compulsion. They include the grain offering, burnt offering, peace offering, sin offering, trespass offering, first fruit harvest, one tenth of the income for the Levites, one tenth for the ingathering of fruits, and one tenth for the poor, to name just a few (Leviticus 1–5, 23:22; Malachi 3:6–12; 2 Kings 4:42–44; Deuteronomy 14:28–29). There are many different methods that Christians today use for giving, but no matter the method, the Christian should always give out of love and not out of compulsion. Everywhere in the Bible, miserliness, greed, and avarice are denounced, and generosity, hospitality, and love are extolled. These giving principles should always be kept in mind, no matter the method used.

By pledging

Pledging is one of the methods in which believers today give unto the Lord. This involves making a promise unto God that one will give a certain amount for the work of the Gospel. When one has pledged, it is now a sort of obligation for the pledger to fulfill that pledge. Where one fails to do so, church officials can help remind the giver.

Although there are no clear New Testament examples of pledging, Christians are free to use this method, and as we shall see, there may be some practical reasons for doing so. If that is the case, one needs to be careful before pledging, so that one may not become a debtor when one fails to fulfill the pledge.

The pledge may involve setting apart a certain amount each day, week, month, or year for the Lord's work. The amount given should be proportionate to one's income and also something worthy of the giver and of the giver's love for the Master. It should be appropriate to the sacrifices that those who conduct the specific ministry are making. The one who pledges should keep in mind that the spiritual blessings that come from being generous in God's work are far more valuable than the financial gain that is made by refusing to give.

There are several practical ways that pledging can benefit a church or ministry:

1. *Pledging empowers identity.* A pledge card is given to every individual in the congregation for his or her pledge, regardless of the amount. This shows solidarity with the family of believers. The John Creek Baptist Church states, "A pledge card says, 'We believe in what we are doing as a church and in who we are becoming together in Christ.' A pledge card says 'Yes. We're in.'"[67]
2. *Pledging empowers accountability.* When someone pledges, he or she creates for himself or herself a method of accountability. When you pledge, you empower your church to empower you.

3. *Pledging empowers the ministry budget.* A church budget enhances the church's funding plan. Through prayer, the ministers, deacons, stewardship committee, treasurers, and other leaders develop the church budget that the church depends upon each year. Pledges given in advance help them plan effectively. The John Creek Baptist Church explains this further:

> Our treasurer equips us with an intelligent analysis of trends from week to week, month to month, and year to year. But one vital tool used is the total number of pledges submitted from a faithful and consistent membership. When you pledge, you help our leadership responsibly discern the viability funding the ministry initiatives being envisioned.[68]

Rev. Lisa G. Fischbeck, a vicar in Chapel Hill, North Carolina, comments on pledging in the Episcopal Café website:

> Pledging has little to do with stewardship. Rather, it has to do commitment and with budget planning. To pledge to a particular organization is to make a commitment to support that organization. When people are able to estimate their giving ahead of time and pledge a particular amount, then the leadership of the church is able to determine a budget for the year and establish certain commitments and expectations.[69]

Believers can greatly assist their individual churches and the different organizations that they support by pledging and then fulfilling their pledges.

By almsgiving

Besides pledging, we still have almsgiving as another method of giving. "Almsgiving means benevolent giving: money or gifts for the relief of the poor."[70] Most religions encourage almsgiving for different reasons:

"The Muslim gives money to a beggar to follow the teachings of the prophet and to earn merit. Other religions encourage people to get rid of as many possessions as possible in order to be free from worldly evil. The Jews are told to give money away as an act of obedience to God, the Creator of all and the giver of all good gifts. Christians too give alms as an act of obedience to God... The true Christian, whether he gives to his church, or to other people, gives his money as an outward and visible sign that he gives his love."[71] The Compelling Truth website give some of the Old Testament background on almsgiving: "In the Bible and in historic Christianity, almsgiving was the act of filling a material need for someone less fortunate, usually by giving money. God incorporated the concept of alms into the Mosaic Law when He ordered land-owners to leave to the poor the corners of the fields (Leviticus 19:9–10)."[72] The land was to lie fallow every seventh year (Exodus 23:11), and the gleanings from the harvest were to be left for poor in the field and vineyard (Leviticus 23:22, Ruth 2:2–8).

Refusing to give alms to the poor brought retribution (Proverbs 21:13), so almsgiving is essential for all believers. Jesus taught that Christians should give alms in the Sermon on the Mount (Matthew 6:1–4) and in His prediction of judgment for the Gentiles (Matthew 25:31–36, 42–45).

By thanksgiving
Thanksgiving is another way of expressing our gratefulness towards God and man. It shows our heart's gratitude and appreciation for what we have received. The Psalms encourage us to be thankful to God in many, many passages: "Give thanks to him, and praise his name" (Psalm 100:4). In fact, entire psalms are devoted to thanking God! For instance, David gives thanks unto God at length in the marvelous Psalm 103. We need to follow his example of thankfulness.

Many people have survived sicknesses and therefore have praised God by giving cash or something of value for what He has done. Others have received gifts of the womb and have praised God through their giving as well. In a host of ways, God has blessed mankind, and mankind has seen the need to return thanks unto God. The example of one of the ten lepers healed by Jesus in Luke 17:11–19 is very familiar to us. He was commended by Christ for returning thanks unto Him, while the other nine were not commended because they failed to come back to give thanks. And the expression of our gratefulness in praise often attracts further blessings. That is why the Igbo people of Nigeria said, "If you thank someone for the good thing he has done, he will be motivated to do more next time."

By giving anonymously
Be careful not to practice your righteousness before men to be seen by them. If you do, you will have no reward from your Father in heaven. So, when you give to the needy, do not announce it with trumpets, as the hypocrites do in the synagogues and on the streets, to be honored by men. I tell the truth; they have received their reward in full. But when you give to the needy, do not let your left hand know what your right hand is doing, so that your giving may be in secret. Then your Father, who sees what is done in secret, will reward you. (Matthew 6:1–4)

Jesus encourages us to give secretly so that God will reward us openly. It will protect the giver from been spiritually proud of what he has done. Anderson wrote, "This kind of giving is preferable as it protects the giver from spiritual pride. When giving directly to someone, we should look for ways to meet a need without the beneficiary ever knowing who gave the money."

By giving expectantly
Believers are to give expecting blessings from the Lord. The more we give generously, the more the Lord will bless us. If we give little, we will get little in return. What the Bible says is true: "Remember this: Whoever

sows sparingly will also reap sparingly, and whoever sows generously will also reap generously" (2 Corinthians 9:6). Anderson illustrates this principle in a most memorable fashion:

> When someone sows by scattering seed with an open hand, it looks like he is just throwing away good grain. If he were to grip the seed in his fist, or only cast a seed or two, there would be a very small harvest. So, it is with Christian giving. If we give either nothing or very little, we can expect very little blessing. But if we give with open, generous hand, we expect to reap bountifully.[73]

By tithing?

Having considered the methods of the New Testament giving, one might ask two questions: Should Christians pay tithes, and should all giving be done through the Church?

The tithe was simply a minimum percentage set by God for the Jewish people. The tithe was by no means the ideal of giving even in the Old Testament days. There were all sorts of offerings given to God by the people of Israel over and above their tithe: the cereal offering, burnt offering, freewill offering, and so on. Tithing for the Israelites expressed gratitude too, reminding them that material blessings came from God (Leviticus 1:2, 22:17, 18; Exodus 35:5, 21).

But the word *tithe* is found in the New Testament only eight times (Matthew 23:23; Luke 11:42, 18:22; Hebrews 7:5–6, 8–9), according to Ryrie. In the references in the Gospels, it is used in connection with that which the Pharisees were doing in fulfilling their obligation to the Mosaic law. The references in Hebrews use tithing to prove the inferiority of the Levitical priesthood to the Melchizedek priesthood. So having tithing as a mandatory practice for believers today has no solid New Testament support.[74] Lugt and Smith stated this quite strongly:

> No one should preach tithing as the biblical norm for the amount we should give. Nowhere in both the Old Testament and New Testament is one tenth the exact amount God expects.[75]

A true Christian's giving should be of one's accord, despite afflictions and poverty, out of joy, bountiful, regular, proportionate, sacrificial, and practiced by all. Giving will not be generous, spontaneous and joyful until it is regarded not as a duty, but as a privilege. This can happen only when we are concerned more about the needs of the church and others than we are about our own. This giving should be made in different ways through pledging, almsgiving, and thanksgiving. Our Lord taught us, "It is more blessed to give than to receive" (Acts 20:35).

The Scripture teaches that Christians should give in proportion to their income (1 Corinthians 16:2). This should be done according to one's heart, one's love, and one's purpose. Christians are to realize that tithing is not mandatory in the New Testament. But the principles for Christian giving are similar to the Old Testament directives. Our gifts should still come from grateful hearts, express worship, benefit those ministering to us spiritually, and help the needy.[76]

By giving only to the local church?
Whether tithe or offerings, should one give only to one's local church? This question might be answered by people in different ways. We do have a responsibility to support the leaders who minister to us spiritually in our churches. At the same time, just as our own obligations to serve are not confined to our local church community, we should consider the support of those *outside* the local church who minister to us spiritually and who help meet needs elsewhere. The Philippian support of Paul while he ministered in Corinth allows for giving to ministers who are not part of the local church (2 Corinthians 11:9; Philippians 4:15). And there is clear New Testament precedent for giving to needs outside the local church in Paul's collections for the poor in Jerusalem. (Romans 15:25–27 is one of several passages.) The amount given could be part

of one's tithe or offerings: since the Christian was to give account of the money entrusted into his or her care, then he or she was responsible to decide where best to give (1 Corinthians 4:2, Matthew 25:1–46, Luke 19:11–27).

What Motivates Donors

There are many things that motivate donors to support nonprofits, charities, or religious organizations. Every nonprofit organization or church should show proof of accountability and stewardship of the funds God has entrusted into its care. In the United States, this is a legal requirement, but responsible ministries in other countries should do it also, whether required or not. The accountability and detailed information encourage potential contributors to start supporting your organization. Here are other items that motivate donors:

1. *They share your mission.* When the mission of any organization is well-stated and is well-known, people can more easily buy into the organization. Some donors say, "I know there is a need for the nonprofit's mission in my community and I know it does good work."[22] Take for example, Eternal Word Communication Ministries' mission statement: "To educate Nigerian children academically, spiritually, emotionally, physically in light of the Word of God."
This is the ministry that my wife and I are involved in. Since 1994, when the ministry began, many individuals and churches have bought into our vision and mission and have gotten involved in it. They have tagged along with us since its inception. Some others have joined in our mission along the way. We are most grateful to God for them all.

2. *They trust your organization.* When people trust you and your organization, they can go a long way to supporting what you are doing. But when there is lack of trust, they will not support what you are doing. "Donors come to your nonprofit because they believe in your mission. They stay with you because you prove yourself worthy of their trust and commitment. Transparency and dependability are

key. When you say you're going to do something, be true to your word."[78]
3. *They get to see the impact.* The fact that your ministry is very impactful cannot be overemphasized. They see it in the lives of the people you plan to reach. When this is actualized, your donors will stand with you and other people will join, too. "When donors feel their gift has a direct impact on improving a situation, they feel empowered. Share specifics with your donors about what their gifts support. Detailed information about what you're accomplishing as a direct result of donations gives donors confidence."[79]
4. *They have a personal connection with you.* When donors see or know or hear about someone who has benefitted from your organization, they will be spurred to start giving and continuing to give! The evidence is clear. "Donors who give because they've seen your impact firsthand are incredible advocates for your cause. If you aren't asking donors why they give, you might miss out on these stories and opportunities to spread the word about your mission."[80]
5. *They want to be part of something.* Definitely some people want to be a part of something going on in their community or society, especially things that are going well. "Put a human face to your facts and statistics, and get to the heart of the matter. Share that with your donors, so they can connect with your work on a personal level."[81] That is why the newsletters of most organizations have pictures of the people they are reaching out to.
6. *You've caught their attention.* Many organizations, churches, and companies are on the social media. When they search your web site or blog to find out what you are up to, they can see it. As they say, "One picture *is* worth a thousand words!" "The more people see their peers involved in a cause, the more likely they are to participate and donate. Plus, participating in social campaigns is fun."[82]
7. *They want tax benefits.* The United States government has authorized donations to recognized nonprofit organizations and churches as tax-deductible. Tax deductions reduce the amount of tax they pay

in their yearly earning to the government. That is an encouragement to many donors that may want to participate in your ministry.

Five Reasons We Should Give to Charity or Support Causes We Believe In "But give that which is within as charity, and then all things are clean for you" (Luke 11:41 NASB). It is very important for people to give to causes or organizations they believe in. Not only does giving benefit the charities themselves, it can have positive effects on the givers, too.

1. *Giving to charity make you feel good.* People feel fulfilled when they remember that they are helping out other people in one way or another. "Donating to charity is a major mood-booster. The knowledge that you're helping others is hugely empowering and, in turn, can make you feel happier and more fulfilled. Research has identified a link between making a donation to charity and increased activity in the area of the brain that registers pleasure, proving that as the old adage goes, it really is far better to give than to receive."[83]
2. *Giving to charity strengthens personal values.* People can grow spiritually when they use whatever they have to help others. "Having the power to improve the lives of others is, to many people, a privilege, and one that comes with its own sense of obligation. The feelings of responsibility is a great way to reinforce our own personal values."[84]
3. *Giving to charity is more impactful than ever.* Some people think that their donations might be reduced by tax or administrative costs. The good news is that donations are tax-deductible in many countries. And many are finding ways to make their giving more effective: "There are many other ways to give to charity 'tax-effectively,' such as by donating straight from your salary before tax is deducted, by donating shares in stocks to a charity, or by leaving a charitable legacy in your will."[85]
4. *Giving to charity introduces your children to the importance of generosity.* It is very good to teach your children to know how to give to charity from the early stage of their lives. When they learn it, they will not depart from it. "Starting a tradition of donating to charity with

your children is easy. Try making a donation box that everyone in the family can contribute to, and involve the children in choosing which causes to support."[86]
5. *Giving to charity encourages friends and family to do the same.* If you are used to giving to charity, it is good to encourage your friends and family members to do likewise. "Your own charitable donations can inspire your nearest and dearest to give to causes important to them and could even bring about a family-wide effort to back a charity that has special significance to you as a group."[87]

Some Reasons Why Donors May Stop Supporting Your Organization
There are several reasons people have for stopping donations to the charities they had been supporting previously. For a time, they may have enjoyed giving, and it seemed as if it was "till death do us part." Unfortunately, those feelings sometimes change. Here are some possible reasons why.

1. "I'm not able to afford supporting the organization." Lack of funds or income is one of the reasons donors stop giving.
2. "I don't feel connected to the organization anymore." Some people feel disconnected with the organization they were supporting previously for one reason or the other. This may be due to lack of communication from the charity. Or the donor may just be "looking for new people to connect with, or a new place to plug in, or their interests are evolving."[88]
3. "I have no memory of ever supporting that organization." It happens that some people from time to time forget that they have ever donated or supported an organization previously. This may be as a result of the organization not contacting the person after a while. People may donate to some campaign because of a specific person that had been connected to the organization, perhaps someone they had known personally before the fundraiser. They may "easily remember the person that they supported, but have no recollection of the organization behind the campaign."[89]

4. "They ask me for too much money." Some people think that many churches and other groups ask for too much money all the time. For that reason, people are turned off, and they stop giving to good causes. Charities and organizations should be conscious of that and be cautious about how they ask for support so that they do not to turn off some of their supporters. "Too much asking is a turnoff [which often happens when you ask for too little] and can send donors running for another organization."[20]
5. "They don't tell me how my money is being used." Many donors are always happy when they know how their donations or money is being spent. They are assured that their donations are going for good causes. That makes them continue supporting your organization or ministry. "People want to know that their money is making a difference. If supporters don't understand their impact, they'll find a new place to invest."[21]
6. "They never reminded me to give again." People need to be reminded that your work is ongoing and that their donation is still needed. "This is one of the top reasons donors leave. They never received a message as simple as, 'Thank you for donating last year. Would you like to give again this year?'"[22]
7. "They said something that rubbed me the wrong way." You may write something in your newsletter that your donor didn't like. That kind of thing can turn people off, and they cease to support your ministry. This kind of thing happens from time to time. "Maybe they read a blog post that bothered them, or they heard something at an event that didn't jibe with their values."[23] In this case, there is not much you can do, just pray.
8. "I could no longer afford to give." This kind of thing happens often. Some kind of hardship sets in and a donor is no longer able to support as he or she used to do before. If they can no longer support your mission financially, thank them for what they have done already. And ask them to continue to be part of the ministry by praying!

9. "The founder of the organization passed away." Some people support an organization because they like the founder or a certain leader. When that person passes away, they may stop donating because they don't know how the successors will move forward. This problem might be prevented by some sensitive communication from the organization to its supporters about what they plan for the future.
10. "The charity no longer needs my support."[94] In other cases, some donors stop supporting the organization when they think the organization may not need their support anymore. This happens when they feel that the organization is doing very well and may not need their help any longer.
11. "The charity did not acknowledge my support."[95] Some organizations may forget to acknowledge the receipt of any donations from individuals or churches. When that happens such individuals or churches may cease supporting your charity. You need to write to the individual or church to apologize to them for the oversight! And after writing, pray that God will touch them to resume supporting your ministry once more.

Conclusion

In this chapter, we have dealt with the principles and methods of Christian giving. Believers are exhorted to give out of joy, give despite affliction, give despite poverty, give according to ability, give oneself, give eagerly asking for the opportunity, give of one's own accord, and give generously, cheerfully, bountifully, regularly, proportionately, and sacrificially. The methods of giving include through pledge, almsgiving, thanksgiving, anonymously, and expectantly. This section also dealt with five reasons we should support charity and different reasons why donors leave. The next chapter will deal with the handicaps to Christian giving in many societies.

Reference for Chapter 3

40. Merrill D. Moore, *Found Faithful* (Nashville, Tennessee: Broadman Press, 1953), p. 34.
41. Bishop Azariah, p. 65.
42. Buttrick, et al. eds, *The Interpreter's Bible. vol. 10* (Nashville, Tennessee: Abingdon Press, 1978), p. 364.
43. Brian Anderson, https://www.thebridgeonline.net/author/brian.
44. Charles Williams, *A Commentary on The Pauline Epistles* (Chicago, Illinois: Moody Press, 1953), p. 202.
45. Buttrick, et al. eds., p. 365.
46. Rice, p. 10.
47. https://www.focusonthefamily.com/family-qa/reasons-christians-dont-give/
48. Buttrick, p. 207.
49. Williams, p. 206.
50. Lugt and Smith, p. 20.
51. Rice, p. 8.
52. https://www.crosswalk.com/family/finances/three-key-principles-of-godly-giving-1426486.html
53. Moore, p. 37.
54. Charles Caldwell Ryrie. *The Ryrie Study Bible*. Chicago, Illinois: Moody Press. 1978, p. 1763.
55. Oswald J. Smith. *The Cry of the World*. London, England: Marshall Morgan and Scott, 1969, p. 65.
56. Williams, p. 207.
57. Anderson, (https://www.thebridgeonline.ne/category/articles/).
58. Charles Ryrie, *The Christian Life*, p. 87.
59. Allen, p. 82.
60. Charles Ryrie, *Christian Life*, p. 86.
61. A. S. Hornby, E. V. Gatenby, H. Wakefield, *The Advanced Learner's Dictionary of Current English* (London, England: Oxford University Press, 1965), p. 67.

62. https://www.biblestudytools.com/bible-study/topical-studies/what-does-the-bible-say- about-giving.html.
63. Charles Ryrie, *Christian Life*, p. 86.
64. https://bible.org/seriespage/lesson-5-giving-god-s-way-selected-scriptures.
65. Ibid, p. 89.
66. https://www.focusonthe family.com/family-qa/biblical-principles-and-principles-about- money/
67. https://jcbc.org/3-reasons-why-pledging-matters/
68. https://jcbc.org/3-reasons-why-pledging-matters/
69. https://www.episcopalcafe.com/stewardship_tithing_giving_annual_pledge_defined/
70. Merrill C. Tenney, Steven Barabas, et al., *The Zondervan Pictorial Encyclopedia of the Bible*. vol. 1 (Michigan: Zondervan Publishing House), 1977, p. 109.
71. Burke, pp. 9–10.
72. https://www.compellingtruth.org/alms.html#:~:text=In the Bible and in historic Christianity%2C almsgiving, seventh year%2C leave the entire field %28E
73. Brian Anderson. (https://www.thebridgeonline.net/authority brian/)
74. Charles Ryrie, *Christian Life*, p. 87.
75. Lugt and Smith, p. 20.
76. Chuck and Winnie Christensen, *We Just Can't Afford to Tithe* (Chicago, Illinois: Moody Monthly. July/August, 1982), p. 91.
77. https://www.networkforgood.com/nonprofitblog/7-reasons-why-donors-give
78. https://www.networkforgood.com/nonprofitblog/7-reasons-why-donors-give
79. https://www.networkforgood.com/nonprofitblog/7-reasons-why-donors-give/
80. https://www.networkforgood.com/nonprofitblog/7-reasons-why-donors-give/
81. https://www.networkforgood.com/nonprofitblog/7-reason-why-donors-give/

82. https://www.networkforgood.com/nonprofitblog/7-reasons-why-donors-give/
83. https://www.cafonline.org/mypersonal-giving-/long-term-giving/resource-centre/five- reasons-to-give-to-charity
84. https://www.cafonline.org/mypersonal-giving-/long-term-giving/resource-centre/five- reasons-to-give-to-charity
85. https://www.cafonline.org/mypersonal-giving-/long-term-giving/resource-centre/five- reasons-to-give-to-charity
86. Ibid.
87. https://www.cafonline.org/my-personal-giving/long-term-giving/resource-centre/five- reasons-to-give--to-charty
88. https://firespring.com/solutions-for-nonprofits/7-reasons-why-donors-leave-you/
89. Hhttps://firespring.com/solutions-for-nonprofits/7-reasons-why-donors-leave-you/
90. https://firespring.com/solutions-for-nonprofits/7-reasons-why-donors-leave-you/
91. https://firespring.com/solutions-for-nonprofits/7-reasons-why-donors-leave-you/
92. https://firespring.com/solutions-for-nonprofits/7-reasons-why-donors-leave-you/
93. https://firespring.com/solutions-for-nonprofits/7-reasons-why-donors-leave-you/
94. www.campbellrinker.com/Managing_donor_defection.pdf
95. Dr. Adrian Sargeant, www.campellrinker.com/Managing_donor_defection.pdf

CHAPTER 4

The Handicaps of Christian Giving in Many Societies

Finances, such an important factor in every organization, corporation, society, and mission, have suffered greatly among Christians due to several reasons. The main problem is that although most of God's people know the motives and purposes of Christian giving, they have not put into practice the principles and methods. Yet there are many other factors that handicap Christian giving.

Poverty

Poverty is one of the reasons people give for their inability to give properly. In some cases, the poverty is due to a lack of employment. In African churches, the shortage of funds is made worse by the extended family system. There every adult is expected to look after a handful of relatives or more, regardless of whether or not the immediate family can afford it.

Many in the United States are unaware of how widespread the problem of poverty is. In fact, most of the Christians of the world are impoverished. Merrill D. Moore, in his book *Found Faithful*, provides some saddening statistics:

> Half of the earth's population receives an average income of less than one hundred dollars per year. Two thirds of the people

live below subsistence level. Men are hungry. More than half of mankind is suffering from malnutrition… The sick are without a physician, medicine, or anyone to help.[26]

Not only are people poor, they have staggering debts to pay that discourage them from supporting God's work. Many of those living in the wealthier western countries now have reached unprecedented levels of debt due to a mortgage, car loan, student loan, or credit card. With many church members enslaved by debts, often due to spending that could have been avoided, they often feel that they cannot give to the Lord.[27]

Granting greater honor to the wealthy
The wealthier people are often accorded much more recognition in churches than the average or the poor ones. Some of these wealthy members are given special front seats where no one else can sit in the church. This segregation violates the clear teaching of Scripture (James 4:1–9). The Bible says that God does not show any partiality to any person (Acts 10:34, Romans 2:11), and we should aim to be like Him in this. But often the pastor and elders are complicit in favoring the wealthy, looking to people rather than God to solve the church's financial woes. An unfortunate by-product of favoring the wealthy is that it minimizes the contributions of others (the *widows* with their *mites*) and discourages those of low and average income from giving.

Imposed giving in the form of Levies
A widespread practice in the churches of many countries is to levy the members in order to collect money for church projects. This is because of the lack of the spirit of giving in such an organization or church. The church will impose certain amounts of money on its members in the form of a class levy, building levy, and harvest levy. These are compulsory, because if a member fails to pay any of these levies and then dies, these levies must be cleared before the church will bury him or her! And as soon as the money is paid, he or she will be considered a

faithful member of the church, even though the person may never have been a true believer! A glorious funeral service will be organized for him or her by the church, in which the deceased is praised and set up as an example.

Such methods may produce more money in the short term, but they do not help to educate the people on Christian principles of giving. Jason Soroski wrote:

> God loves a cheerful giver! This is a beautiful thought because of what Paul says (give cheerfully) and because of what he doesn't say (give a certain amount). God doesn't desire our giving to be done begrudgingly or under compulsion. Should you be pressured to give a certain amount (or else), then there is something very wrong and very non-scriptural happening. That giving has gone from being a joy to a burden.[28]

Lack of budgeting for church needs
The importance of budgeting for any business or mission cannot be overemphasized. Many churches are financially bankrupt due to the lack of sensible budgeting for church needs. Other churches make the mistake of not communicating the budget details to those who attend. The congregation does not know what the church's financial needs are, or what monetary priorities need to be met. When the members are unaware of the church's true financial situation, it will inevitably lead to a lack of sacrificial giving. They will not see their responsibility for the church's needs, and they will they think that their fifty cents or one dollar is enough.

If the church leaders communicate the details of the budget, it will encourage biblical giving. It is also a wise practice to involve the members in the decision-making process for the budget. If the average attenders have more ownership of the decisions, they are more likely to take ownership of fulfilling the budget with their gifts.

Lack of good accounting system in the church
It is not enough for the members to know the budget details for which they contribute to the welfare of the church. It is also very necessary for them to know how their offering has been spent. But in many churches, little or no account is given, and the report may not be accurate.

The members are much more likely to give if the church reports to them how the money is spent. A very common practice is for the church treasurer to give a printed monthly report to the church board and an annual printed report to the entire congregation. The treasurer should be available to welcome questions when the report is presented. It is also a good practice, especially with large churches, to increase accountability by having an outside audit verify that the church bookkeeping is done accurately and honestly.

Embezzlement of church funds
Sometimes the reason that the church leadership is vague about how the donations have been spent is because they do not *want* the accountability! They resist scrutiny because they are not being honest with the Lord's money. The same *pest* that plagues the businesses of unbelievers is eating deeper and deeper in our churches more than ever before. This *pest* is none other than church officials embezzling the money entrusted into their care. *Embezzlement* is a fancy word for robbery in the house of God. The Igbos of Nigeria describe it as "a dog eating the bone that was hung on its neck." It needs to be stopped! "How sad, it is to find Christians not perfectly trustworthy in handling other people's money. Misuse of money wrecks the church's reputation and the individual's soul."[22]

Lack of good Scriptural teaching
The lack of good scriptural teaching on giving today is a principle reason for why so few modern Christians practice biblical stewardship. Most Christians fail to give properly because they are not taught biblical

principles of giving by the church leadership and have not seen Scriptural giving demonstrated in the lives of other members. As a result, people have almost no vision of what proper giving can do in their lives.

Most new churches do not give correct teaching on giving to the people who start attending their services. New Christians are taught that they must give themselves to God, but they are not shown properly that surrender to our Lord must show itself in many specific ways. The leadership shies away from teaching new believers to show their love with gifts, financial and otherwise, made to God, and to the church. They are not taught how, why, and to whom they should give.[100]

The prosperity Gospel preachers are particularly guilty of wrong teaching on giving. Their teaching is that "financial blessing and physical well-being are always the will of God for them, and that faith positive speech and donations to religious causes will increase one's material wealth. Prosperity theology views the Bible as a contract between God and humans; if humans have faith in God, he will deliver security and prosperity."[101] This is a very unscriptural and dangerous teaching! God doesn't owe us anything, and nothing that we can do can obligate God to us. It all depends on God to bless us however He chooses. We cannot force Him against His will.

The solution to this problem is correct teaching by the pastors and minsters of the gospel of Christ. Believers are to be taught the principles of stewardship. Patrick Johnson, citing the teaching of Ron Blue, summarizes the reasons Christians do not give properly: don't plan to, don't know how to, limited relationships, limited vision, financial problems, and spiritual problems. He concludes as follows:

> So let's look at the root issue of why people don't give- spiritual problems. I've talked with many megachurch leaders about what percentage of their weekend attendees don't give anything to the church during a year. The answer I hear most often is 50

percent of the people give $0. Fifty percent! And when I think about these folks, I would guess that they don't read their Bible, pray outside of a crisis, serve others.[102]

Eliot Crowther and Chris Heaslip, co-founders of Pushpay.com, have these suggestions for the clergy on how to educate their members on how to improve on their giving standards: (1) Get your leadership on board. The church leaders and staff need to be committed to the idea. "So whatever amount you encourage your members to give, people in leadership need to demonstrate."[103] (2) Be clear about your expectations. Try to "get people comfortable with thinking about their finances as an extension of their faith." (3) Make giving easy. Some people don't carry their checkbooks or cash with them all the time. Make it possible for them by providing a simple, fast, mobile option that makes giving available for them in a snap. (4) Share giving stories. "They need to hear from people who made the decision to give regularly and about the positive impact it had on their lives."[104] (5) Offer financial classes. This will educate the members on the principles of biblical stewardship so that they will experience firsthand the joys of Christian giving.

Fear
People are afraid of what will happen to their finances if they give because of their limited resources and a host of needs to be met. "There is much fear with finances. When Christians give, they can often withhold or reduce their giving due to fear. They start asking themselves, 'If I give this money, will I be able to pay the kid's school fees, the mortgage, and other bills?'"[105] People should remember that God has promised to meet needs of faithful givers (Philippians 4:19, compare 4:15–18).

Lack of maturity
Many Christians are not mature in their Christian walk, and one way that they show this is in a lack of giving. The church leadership needs to teach the members about spiritual growth, so that they can become strong in their faith. This will include their financial discipleship.

The leaders need to teach about proper stewardship of money and possessions, about the use of money, about giving money, and about how "the love of money is a root of all kinds of evil" (1 Timothy 6:10).

"Each of us are at a different stage of our Christian maturity. The challenge for church leaders is to effectively disciple the members to become Christ-centered mature followers of Jesus. Don't forget financial discipleship. Our giving is a litmus test of our spiritual maturity. In fact, our bank statements are like theological documents as they tell us about what we really believe."[106]

It's all mine anyway; why should I give?
Most people labor under the mistaken notion that they are the true owners of their money and possessions. They forget that we are all merely stewards of what the Lord has entrusted to us. And we are only temporary stewards at that. Everything we supposedly *own* actually belongs to God. The Lord states, "For every animal of the forest is mine, and the cattle on a thousand hills" (Psalm 50:20).

The Bible says, "The earth is the Lord's and everything in it, the world, and all who live in it" (Psalm 24:1). For that reason, what we supposedly "give," is actually the Lord's. So we are "giving" something that is only on loan to us in the first place. Therefore, we should learn how to give generously. There are so many rewards in giving.

My gifts don't really count
Some people may think that because they don't have a lot of money that their money doesn't really count. But the widow in the Gospels was recognized not because of the amount of money she gave but because of the heart with which she gave.

Jesus sat down opposite the place where the offerings were put and watched the crowd putting their money into the temple treasury. Many rich people threw in large amounts. But a poor widow came and put in two very small copper coins, worth only a few cents. Calling his disciples to him, Jesus said, "I tell you the truth, this poor widow has put more into the treasury than all the others. They all gave out of their wealth; but she, out of her poverty, put in everything—all she had to live on" (Mark 12:41–44).

We should not wait to give until we had much to give. If we wait, we may never give to God. Whatever we give to God will count no matter how little or how big it is, as long as it comes from a cheerful heart.

Conclusion

We have investigated different points on many handicaps that hinder people from giving to God and His ministry. Some of those problems include poverty, granting more recognition to the wealthy, coercion through levies, lack of responsible accounting, lack of budgeting, lack of scriptural teaching, lack of maturity, thinking you will not have enough, thinking that the money is really yours, and thinking that one's gifts don't really count. But these problems do have answers, and in our next chapter, we will consider what some of those solutions are.

Reference for Chapter 4

96. Moore, p. 4.
97. https://wealthwithpurpose.com/our-courses/
98. https://www.biblestuytools.com/bible-study/topical-studies/what-does-the-bible-say-about- giving.html.
99. Bishop Azariah, p. 55.
100. Bishop Azariah, p. 28.
101. En.m.wikipedia.org.
102. Hhttps://churchleaders.com/pastors-/pastor-how-to/150313 patrick-johnson-giving-why- christians-don-t-give-church.html.
103. https://pushpay.com/blog/20-bible-verses-about-tithing/
104. https://pushpay.com/blog/20-bible-versse-about-tithing/
105. https://wealthwithpurpose.com/our-course/
106. https://wealthwithpurpose.com/our-course/

Chapter 5

Solutions to the Lack of Christian Giving

Though there are many handicaps to Christian giving in our churches, there are solutions to such problems. They include giving despite one's poverty, removing imposed levies, budgeting for the needs of the church or ministry, proper accounting, encouraging indigenous ways of giving, and good scriptural teaching on giving.

Giving despite poverty
Poverty is not an adequate answer for why there is a lack of sacrificial giving amongst Christians. This is because no matter what one's financial standard is, one can still give his widow's mite just like the poor widow (Mark 12:41–44) or like the Macedonian Christians did (2 Corinthians 8:1–5). And if an individual is unemployed or has no money coming in, that person can still contribute her or his time, skills, or service to the Lord's work. The example of the parable of the talents should motivate us to give no matter what our financial standing might be, knowing full well that we are accountable for what has been entrusted to us (Matthew 25:14–30).

Giving should be voluntary instead of being imposed
Methods of raising money for the Lord's work by coercion need to be done away with once and forever. These include the high-pressure use of the class levy, harvest levy, building levy, bazaars, assessments, or Annual

Missionary Collection (AMC). These tactics do not make the allowance for people to give proportionately, voluntarily, or sacrificially. They actually *prevent* believers from giving according to biblical principles. Buttrick wrote, "When appealing for money, let the ambassador for Christ seek to awaken in people the imaginative sympathy and love from which liberality springs, and not induce them to give because of their personal loyalty to himself."[107]

Or as Jesus said, "Freely you have received; freely give" (Matthew 10:8).

The need of budgeting
The need for budgeting cannot be overemphasized. Even Jesus asked, "Suppose one of you wants to build a tower. Won't you first sit down and estimate the cost to see if you have enough money to complete it? For if you lay the foundation and are not able to finish it, everyone who sees it will ridicule you, saying, 'This person began to build and wasn't able to finish'" (Luke 14:28). The idea of planning ahead of time is embedded in Jesus's parable.

The budget will help the church or ministry see the areas where it needs to put its money. A good budget includes plans to secure funds to meet the needs in the church's programs. There should be a control in the distribution to assure that the instructions of the church are carried out and that the money will be spent only as it was received. The budget gives the church the necessary control over expenditures. It helps to train the members in meeting their responsibility. It helps to plan to reach the unreached and minister to the needs of God's people. And when the budget for the entire year is met, it will produce a testimony as to the faithfulness of God.

There are some consequences of not budgeting. Lack of a budget makes it much more difficult to achieve the church's ministry goals. "With a budget, you can easily plan your spending and cut expenses to achieve that goal. On top of that, if you continually track your expenses, you will be able to identify when your spending is drifting off course, and what you need to do to fix it."[108] Other consequences are lack of savings, less financial control, overspending, debt, stress, and being overwhelmed by unexpected expenses. The author of *Painful Consequences of Not Budgeting* concludes, "I think the overarching consequence of not budgeting is an increase in stress. Think about it: whether you're unprepared for unexpected expenses, or you feel like you've lost financial control, or you spend beyond your means, or you're buried in debt and you're unfilled with your financial life, it's stressful."[109]

A financial budget committee should be set up. They should study the areas of need of the church, as stated above. There should be a current budget column, a benevolence, and a missionary budget column. They should draw up a tentative budget, study it, and give recommendations. The tentative budget should be presented to the elders and deacons for their study. Finally the approved budget will be presented to the entire church. It needs to spend only that which is approved in the budget or the subsequent church action.[110]

The budget idea in church finance is a great advancement. Through it, the church will enable its givers to know clearly at the beginning of the year what they might expect. And the multiplicity of unpleasant financial appeals in the Sunday morning services will be reduced and eventually disappear.

A good accounting system
A good accounting system depends largely on the leaders that are the elders or bishops of the church. Make sure that they are not greedy (1 Timothy 3:3). Paul recommended Titus and his colleagues because they were tested and proven leaders who would not embezzle the church's funds.

All offerings should be counted and entered in the account book as soon as the service is over, and in the presence of more than one representative member of the congregation. They should make sure that the whole amount is regularly paid into the church treasury and not used by the pastor or lay workers as part advance on salary. The church or organization should maintain basic records, such as summary of receipts, individual donor records, a checkbook, and an account with a local bank.

The pastors and other leaders should be absolutely scrupulous and beyond reproach in handling any church money. Monthly reports to the official church boards are necessary and an annual report for the entire church body.[111] "An annual statement of the contributions of the people and how they have been disbursed creates confidence, increases interest, and helps further sacrificial giving."[112]

Encourage indigenous ways of giving
It is true that many Christians in the world want to give but do not have the cash to give. They should be encouraged to give material things like bananas, oranges, yams, rice, beans, etc., which they have produced. If the offering has too much food at one time, such produce could be sold and converted into cash for other purposes. It could be given to the less privileged ones in the church. Others could give by working in the church instead of giving money. "Money is the medium of exchange. It represents your labor, your skill, your sweat and effort—your whole self. When you give it, you give yourself."[113] The church needs to be a place where every member can give according to the Holy Spirit's guidance.

There are multiple options for how the church can conduct the offering. This could be done while people come into the church or while going out or during a special time set aside during the service. It could be done even in secret when no other person is watching. A church can set up a permanent offering box into which people can contribute at different times. Some churches use multiple boxes, marked for donations to the poor, missions, ministry, and other purposes.

The Joy of Faithful and Cheerful Giving

Clear Scriptural teaching on giving

Jesus's instruction to his disciples to go into all nations, teaching them to observe all things whatsoever He has commanded them is an imperative (Matthew 28:20).[114] If we cannot be excused for failing to teach the doctrines of atonement, of salvation, and of the church, in the same way we cannot be excused for failing to teach the doctrine of stewardship.

Churches that have neglected to teach biblical giving should be awakened to a deeper experience of the Christian life and to faithful teaching on stewardship according to New Testament principles. Converts should be taught the duty and privilege of Christian stewardship from the very beginning of their Christian life. Waldo Werning wrote:

> Only scriptural principles will produce scriptural giving habits. You cannot sow self and reap the spirit. The solution to lack of giving is not to collect stewardship verses and inject them into Christians to get them to yield what the church needs, but to teach the Gospel so that the Holy Spirit knocks down human barriers in the hearts and builds a house of love in the same place.[115]

Jason Soroski's comments on Christian giving should encourage every believer:

> Throughout the centuries, Christians have given generously and sacrificially for the cause of the Gospel. Christians have funded schools, charities, and hospitals. Christians have given time and treasure to rebuild cities after floods and fires. Christians have given faithfully to their local churches, to missionaries, to neighbors in need, and have given consistently in ways that others will never know. Following the lead of our Savior who gave all on our behalf, Christians are a giving people.[116]

Conclusion

The question of giving is not a sad one as many people think; rather, it is a joyful one. Even though many people fail to give generously, proportionately, voluntarily, cheerfully, and sacrificially, it is still good to realize that there are blessings in giving (Acts 20:35).

For this reason, Christ's noble example should motivate every Christian to give sacrificially for the Lord's work and to the less privileged ones.

Not only Christ's example should motivate us into giving but the realization that all the material possessions and social opportunities that have come to us are actually entrusted to us from God. This realization should stimulate us to give to Him in return.

Where biblical giving has been hindered by poverty, embezzlement, lack of budgeting, or other obstacles, we need to correct the problems with good scriptural teaching and sensible practices!

Biblical giving produces honor to God, expresses our gratitude to Christ, yields Christian character, produces spiritual joy, and meets the spiritual, emotional, and physical needs of people everywhere. And of course, giving more than a tithe is much better. It is the writer's prayer that reading this book will help his audience to become better stewards of their possessions and more joyful servants of Christ.

Reference for Chapter 5

107. Buttrick et al., p. 367.
108. https://bethebudget.com/consequences-of-not-budgeting/#:~:text=8
     https://bethebudget.com/consequences-of-not-budgeting text=8
109. Moore, pp. 64–65.
110. Kenneth K. Kilinski and Jerry C. Wofford, *Organization and Leadership in the Local Church* (Grand Rapids; Michigan: Zondervan Publishing House, 1976), p. 199.
111. Bishop Azariah, p. 89.
112. Oral Roberts, *Miracle of Seed Faith* (Tulsa, Oklahoma: Oral Roberts, 1970), p. 20.
113. Delonise M. Beall, *Christian Stewardship* (Grand Rapids, Michigan: Zondervan Publishing House), 1955.
114. Waldo J. Werning, *What Moves Men as Stewards* (*Christianity Today*. April 24, 1970), p. 91.
115. www.Jasonsoroski.wordpress.com

Appendix

I heartily recommend the article *50 Ways to Encourage Faithful Giving* Lewis Center for Church Leadership of Wesley Theological Seminary.

The article can be accessed at https://www.churchleadership.com/50-ways/50-ways-to-encourage-faithful-giving/ and is reprinted here by permission. The article exhorts individual Christians and Christian organizations to grow in discipleship through faithful stewardship and extravagant generosity. I have reproduced the entire article here and encourage all the readers of this book to read this section of the appendix.

Stress the spiritual dimension of stewardship
1. Teach stewardship as a holistic model of our relationship with God, as the tangible expression of our trust in God. Giving is spiritual matter as central to faithful living as prayer, Bible study, and worship.
2. As act of worship. Use the offering time to lift the spiritual significance of giving. Take an offering at every service.
3. Set a good example. The pastor should tithe and encourage other ministers, staff, and leaders to do the same. All leaders must take their giving seriously and model generosity.
4. Talk openly about money and faithfulness to God. If leaders are uncomfortable about money, then members will be also. Know your story of giving and be willing to testify about it.

5. Model the giving spirit you seek from members in your church budget by giving generously to ministries beyond the congregation.
6. Teach the theology of stewardship through a variety of means-church school classes, other study venues, sermons, and correspondence. Use stewardship scriptures, quotations, and stories in bulletins, newsletters, other printed materials, and the websites.

Know what motivates giving

7. Know that people give to many things for a variety of reasons. Few have a well-planned or consistent giving strategy. Some give on impulse. Others are more cautious. Different kinds of appeals re effective with different types of givers.
8. Recognize that people want to make a difference. They will give to what they value.
9. Appreciate that faithful giving is a fruit of spiritual maturity. It takes time and much nurture to develop.
10. Do not engage in fund raising. People give to God, not to raise the preacher's salary or pay the utilities. Don't make church gifts 'one more bill to pay"—a bill that can be skipped without late fees, penalties, or the need to catch-up. Emphasizing giving as a joyful response to God's generosity, not an obligation.
11. Talk to members about stewardship and opportunities for giving. Most people never increase their giving because they were asked, nor given compelling reasons to do so. Don't be afraid to lift the needs of the church, but always in a way that emphasizes mission.
12. Nurture relationships. People give to persons and organizations where they feel a connection. Church leaders should listen carefully for clues about issues of importance to church members. Personal solicitation is critical, especially for lager gifts.
13. Remember that people—especially younger generations—give to support mission, not institutions or budgets. Everything you communicate about giving should stress ministry, not maintenance.

14. Congregational vitality is key to giving. Whatever increases member involvement and participation will help giving. Involve as many as possible in the church's ministries.
15. Share information freely about the wonderful things giving makes possible. Use announcements to remind people of the impact they are having. Bulletin boards featuring how the church is in mission are good reminders to a congregation.

Websites offer ways to tell the church's story and to interpret stewardship and giving.

Know your givers and congregational giving patterns
16. Do not make assumptions about what people give—most of the time you will be wrong.
17. Give your pastor access to members' giving records as a matter of pastoral care, not power or privilege'
18. Keep alert for any changes in giving patterns—if giving stops without explanation, if an adult child starts writing checks for their parents, if there is confusion about giving, if designated gifts replace general giving etc. Notify the pastor of any potential pastoral care concerns.
19. Know your people and approach them where they are. Someone who has never given does not respond in the same manner as someone who gives faithfully, proportionately, and generously.
20. Understand the financial profiles in your community. If few people carry cash, a spur of the moment offering will not succeed. Remember that more women than men carry a checkbook and younger generations are younger generations are more inclined to pay by electronic or other non-cash means. A twenty-five-year-old is unlikely to make a stock gift, while an older member on a fixed income may prefer an estate gift to one that reduces their monthly income.
21. Monitor giving indicators throughout the year. Compare pledge payments with those of previous years.

22. Know how actual income compares to budgeted income for a given time of the year. Avoid reporting what is "needed to date" by diving the total budget into equal monthly or weekly segments. No congregation receives its income so evenly. Instead, determine how much income is "needed to date" based on a rolling three-year average of what percent of total giving is normally received during that period.

Provide a variety of ways to give

23 Give people multiple opportunities to give. Those new to the church may be unfamiliar with the concept of pledging and tithing. Other ways of giving can get them in the habit.
24. Consider sending some appropriate communication a few times a year to those who do not pledge and to non-resident members.
25. Remember that people can give from their income, from their assets (stock, 401ks, bonds and real property), or through legacies or bequests. Create giving opportunities appropriate to each type of gift.
26. Don't wait decades between capital campaigns. More frequent capital drives create a culture of supporting the church's capital needs and prevent neglect of property concerns.
27. Create a foundation or permanent fund, even if you have not yet received any bequests. People cannot give to what does not exist. Formulate policies for wills, legacies, and bequests. A large estate gift can be divisive if proper procedures are not in place.

Assist members in the stewardship of their personal resources

28. Remember that personal finances and spending decisions are as much a part of Christian stewardship as giving to the church. Too often churches ask people to consider the church's financial situation, but seldom offer to help with member's financial situations.
29. Teach members to think about their finances as an expression of faith. Use appropriate study resources to foster a theology of

personal stewardship. Reinforce tithing and "first-fruits" giving as a faithful way of prioritizing one's personal finances-not a way to pay church bills.

30. Offer workshops on budgeting, financial management, and estate planning.
31. Encourage sessions in which members can come together to discuss personal financial challenges. For example, parents of students preparing for college could discuss educational funding options. Those responsible for aging parents could come together to talk with other members who have learned resources to help.
32. Minister to the economic concerns of parishioners. Provide pastoral assistance and support groups for the unemployed, those in career transition, and those facing financial difficulty.

Develop a year-round, comprehensive stewardship program

33. Preach stewardship sermons throughout the year, not just in the weeks before asking for an estimate of annual giving.
34. Know that developing a congregation of faithful givers does not happen during a three to four-week stewardship drive. People do not become faithful stewards in one moment or though one influence.
35. Create an annual stewardship calendar, emphasizing different stewardship concerns at different times of year— such as annual commitment in the fall, second mile giving at the year-end, planned giving at All Saints Day, etc. Develop stewardship themes that fit with different church events and liturgical seasons.
36. Encourage faithful giving over the summer by preaching on stewardship the last Sunday before school is out. Everyone knows the churches bills do not go on vacation, so quit reminding your members of that.
37. Make giving and stewardship education a part of your ministry with children and youth.

38. Take the time to do everything related to stewardship well. Poor planning results in poor giving. Inspire generosity through sound management.
39. Know that people give to healthy organizations where they know their money is used wisely.
40. Exhibit honesty and openness in financial interactions.
41. Seek a good working relationship based on trust between the pastor, treasurer, and financial secretary.
42. Make sure at least two unrelated people count the offering each week.
43. Make sure all funds are administered properly. Keep precise records of income and disbursements. Keep your giving records secure.
44. Keep the congregation informed of financial matters in meaningful ways. Issue timely financial reports and make them available to any member who requests them. Report financial concerns in a consistent manner.
45. Send out pledge reports/giving statements in a timely fashion, always with a thank you and a reminder about any update that may be needed.
46. Arrange for an independent audit or review of funds annually. Put a brief announcement in the Sunday bulletin a few times stating the completed audit has been reviewed by the finance committee and is available to members wishing to review it.

Say thanks often

47. Find multiple occasions and ways to say "thank you" to those who make the church's ministry possible-from the pulpit, in person, in the newsletter, and on their giving statements.
48. Conduct annual "thank-a-thon" not associated with a fund drive.
49. Tell stories of how lives are changed because of their giving. People need to know their giving makes a difference.

50. As a sign of appreciation, make sure all your procedures for giving are as convenient as possible. Avoid procedures and policies that are for the convenience of those who handle the funds rather than those who give the funds.[117]

---

117 — A free e-newsletter from the Lewis Center for Church Leadership of Wesley Theological Seminary available at churchleadership.com

WAYS TO GIVE

There are different ways people can give their donations or offerings to churches or organizations or charities. These ways simplify ways people can give from the convenience of their home, church, or business.

Give with a link. Just share a link, and anyone can give without even creating an account.

On your website. Add a prominent button to give on your website. Joanna wrote: "Go digital by adding giving options to your church website. Set up a clear way to offer online giving to your community. This way, they can easily log on your church website to donate from home or even pull out their phones and give right from their seats during a service."[118]

Text to give. A few thumb taps is all it takes.

Kiosk giving. Set up an iPad so they can give in the lobby.

Customizable app. Give through an app you customize to fit your church's look.

Cash and check. You can quickly log your gifts later.

---

118 Joanna Gray, www.clovergive.com

Zelle. You can zelle your gifts or donations or offerings from your account to the church's account or ministry's account or organization's account.

Make it recurring. People can set up a recurring or automatic withdrawal from their accounts monthly. "Those are the benefits of recurring payment options, and the same can be available to congregation when you make that option for giving to your church. Emphasize the option to choose a recurring donation on your website. Allow your congregation the option to schedule their contributions using their debit card right there on your site."[119]

Put someone in charge. Churches and organizations should place people in charge of collecting church offerings and donations. This should be a voluntary job. Their sole responsibility is tracking the money coming into the church or organization. They should also track on how the money is being spent.

---

[119] Joanna Gray, www.clovergive.com

BIBLIOGRAPHY

Commentaries
Buttrick, George A. et al. *The Interpreter's Bible*. vol. 10. Nashville; Tennessee: Abingdon Press, 1978.
Spence, H. D. M., Joseph S. Exell. *The Pulpit Commentary on Corinthians*, vol. 19. Grand Rapids, Michigan: Eerdmans Publishing Company, 1952.
Williams, Charles. *A Commentary on the Pauline Epistles*. Chicago, Michigan: Moody Press, 1953.

Dictionaries and encyclopedias
Hornby, A.S.E.V. Gatenby, H. Wakefield. *The Advanced Learner's Dictionary of Current English*. London: England: Oxford University Press, 1965.
Merrill, Tenney C. et al. *The Zondervan Pictorial Encyclopedia of the Bible*. vol. 1. Grand Rapids, Michigan: Zondervan Publishing House, 1977.

Books
Allen, Hattie Bell. *Living for Jesus*. Nashville, Tennessee: The Sunday School Board of the Southern Baptist Convention, 1939.
Aluko S. A. *Christianity and Communism: The Challenge to Our Church*. Ibadan, Nigeria: Daystar Press, 1964.
Azariah, V. S. *Christian Giving*. New York, New York: World Christian Books Association Press, 1955.

Beall, Delouise M. *Christian Stewardship*. Grand Rapids, Michigan: Zondervan Publishing House, 1955.

Beaven, A. W. *Putting the Church on a Full Time Basis*. New York, New York: Double Day, Doran and Company, Inc., 1928.

Benson, Clarence H. *The Church at Work*. Los Angeles, California: The Viola Book Room, 1929.

Burke, R. M. *Pounds and Pennies: How to Save, Spend and Give Money*. Ibadan, Nigeria: Daystar Press, 1967.

Kilinski, Kenneth K., and Jerry C. Wofford. *Organization and Leadership in the Local Church*. Grand Rapids, Michigan: Zondervan Publishing House, 1976.

Lang, G. H. *An Ordered Life*. London, England: The Paternoster Press, 1959.

Lugt, Vander Herbert and Carl H. Smith. *As the Ushers Come Forward*. Grand Rapids, Michigan: Radio Bible, 1976.

Moore, D. Merrill. *Found Faithful: Christian Stewardship in Personal and Church Life*. Nashville, Tennessee: Broadman Press, 1953.

Rees, Paul S. *Christian Commit Yourself*. London, England: Pickering and Inglis Ltd., 1957.

Rice, R. John. *All About Christian Giving*. Wheaton, Illinois: Sword of the Lord Publishers, 1954.

Roberts, Oral. *Miracle of Seed Faith*. Tulsa, Oklahoma: Oral Roberts, 1970.

Ryrie, Caldwell Charles. *Balancing the Christian Life*. Chicago, Illinois: Moody Press, 1981.

Ryrie, Caldwell Charles. *The Ryrie Study Bible*. Chicago, Illinois: Moody Press, 1978.

Ryrie, Caldwell Charles. *What You Should Know About Social Responsibility*. Chicago, Illinois: Moody Press, 1982.

Sankey, DR. Ira. *Sacred Songs and Solos*. London, England: Marshall Morgan and Scott, "n.d."

Periodicals

Christensen, Winnie and Chuck, "We Just Can't Afford to Tithe."

Mood Monthly. July/August 1982.

Werning, J. Waldo. "What Moves Men as Stewards." *Christianity Today.* 24:91, April 1970.

Some suggested books
Collins, Marjorie A. *Who Cares About the Missionary?* Chicago, Illinois: Moody Press, 1974.
Ely, Virginia. *Stewardship: Witnessing for Christ.* Westwood, New Jersey: Fleming H. Revell Company, 1962.
Harlow, E. R. *The Imperfect Church.* Ontario, Canada: Everyday Publications Inc. M IS 4L7, 1982.
Hillis, Don. *30 Pieces of Silver.* Findlay, Ohio: Durham Publishing Company, 1960.
Legsters, L. L. *God's Fellow-Workers.* Philadelphia, Pennsylvania: Pioneer Mission Agency, 1937.
Sanders Oswald. J. *Light on Life's Problems.* London, Edinburgh: Marshall, Morgan and Scott Limited, 1946.
Smith, B. Paul. *World Conquest.* London, England: Marshall, Morgan and Scott Limited, 1966.
Thompson, Phyllis. *Proving God, Financial Experiences of the China Inland Mission.* Chicago, Illinois: Moody Press, 1956.

Websites
Anderson. https://www.the bridgeonline.ne/category/articles/
Anderson, Brian. https://www.thebridgeonline.net/authority/brian/
Copeland, Kenneth. "Tithing 101: The Top 10 Bible Truths You Need to Know." https://blog.kcm.org/tithing-101-the-top-10-bible-truths-you-need-to-know/?
Cree, Chris. "2 Ways God Promises to Benefit You for Tithing" https://newcreeations.org/god-promises-benefits-tithing/?
Dr. Sargeant, Adrian. www.campellrinker.com/Managing_donor_defection.pdf
En.m.wikipedia.org.
Gray, Joanna. www.clovergive.com

A free e-newsletter from the Lewis Center for Church Leadership of Wesley Theological Seminary available at churchleadership.com
https://bible.org/seriespage/lesson-5-giving-god-s-way-selected-scriptures
https://bible-truths-revealed.com/adv15.html https://blog.kcm.org/tithing-101-the-10-bible-truths-you-need-to-now/?gclid=EAlalQobChMl2rfVfmJ7AlV7Vrx6tBh38ogx7EAMYASAEgL72vD_BwE
https://churchleaders.com/pastors-/pastor-how-to/150313-patrick-johnson-giving-why-christians-don-t-give-church.html.
hhttps://firespring.com/solutions-for-nonprofits/7-reasons-why-donors-leave-you/
https://jcbc.org/3-reasons-why-pledging-matters/
https://pushpay.com/blog/20-bible-verses-about-tithing/ https://ststephens-spokane.com/Ministry/christian-giving-and-pledging.html https://wealthwithpurpose.com/our-course/
https://www.biblestuytools.com/bible-study/topical-studies/what-does-the-bible-say-about-giving.html
https://www.cafonline.org/my-personal-giving/long-term- giving/resource-centre/five-reasons-to-give--to-charty https://www.compellingtruth.org/alms.html#:~:text=In the Bible and in historic Christianity%2C almsgiving, seventh year%2C leave the entire field %28E
https://www.episcopalcafe.com/stewardship_tithing_giving_annual_pledge_defined/
https://www.focusonthefamily.com/family-qa/biblical-principles-and-principles-about-money/
https:www.jerrysavelle.org https://www.networkforgood.com/nonprofitblog/7-reasons-why-donors-give/
https://bethebudget.com/consequences-of-not-budgeting/#:~:text=8 painful Consequences Of Not Budgeting, budgeting%2C
I operated my finances MacArthur, John. "Principles of Godly Giving,

Pt. 1-2 Corinthians 8 & 9"
https:/gracebibleny.org/principles_of_godly_giving_pt_1_2_corinthians_8_9.
Soroski, Jason. "The Way I See It." www.Jasonsoroski.wordpress.com
Val Boyle https://bible-truths-revealed.com/adv15.html
Werning, Waldo J. "What Moves Men as Stewards." Christianity Today. April 24, 1970, p. 91.
www.campbellrinker.com/Managing_donor_defection.pdf

ABOUT THE AUTHOR

Vincent Onyebuchi Nwankpa, PhD, co-founded Eternal Word Communication Ministries with his wife, Chinyere. Vincent loves children. He is the proprietor of Eternal Word Christian Schools International, Umudibia, Nekede, Imo State, Nigeria. He is a retired educator with Los Angeles Unified School District. He is a missionary, a pastor, and a teacher. He has planted churches in Nigeria and USA. He started Eternal Word Christian Church, Nekede. He loves the Lord, Jesus Christ, and loves to serve Him. Dr. Nwankpa serves as elder and board member of his church—Long Beach Alliance Church.

He loves winning souls for Christ. He preaches at Long Beach Rescue Mission once a month. He is a published author of *Understanding Cultural Perspectives, God's Word and Missions: A Powerful Tool for Theologizing* an e-book made simply for you. His other book on marriage is on the way. Dr. Nwankpa is happily married for thirty-six years to his wife, Chinyere, and God has blessed them with two children, Chidi and Chioma. He works for Los Angeles Unified School and Lynwood Unified School District as a substitute teacher when he is not on the mission field overseas in Nigeria.

www.ingramcontent.com/pod-product-compliance
Lightning Source LLC
Chambersburg PA
CBHW070519030426
42337CB00016B/2029